Published in Australia in 2010
by Hardie Grant Books
85 High Street
Prahran, Victoria 3181, Australia
www.hardiegrant.com.au

Published in the United Kingdom in 2010
by Hardie Grant Books (London)

First published in New Zealand in 2009
by Beatnik Publishing in association with Dulcie May Kitchen Ltd

Cataloguing-in-Publication data is available from the National Library of
Australia.

ISBN 978-1-740-66930-6

Food styling by Michelle Burrell
Design and Typesetting by Beatnik Design Ltd, Auckland
Cover reproduction by Splitting Image Colour Studio
Cover design by Michelle Mackintosh
Printed and bound in China by 1010 Printing International Ltd

10 9 8 7 6 5 4 3 2

GRAN'S KITCHEN

Recipes from the notebooks of Dulcie May Booker

NATALIE OLDFIELD

PHOTOGRAPHY BY SALLY GREER

Food Styling by Michelle Burrell

hardie grant books

MELBOURNE · LONDON

Gran,

This book is dedicated to you in thanks for the inspiration you are to me. I have watched you over the years enrich so many lives, not only in your family but within your community and beyond. You have a unique natural grace about you and your inner strength seems unstoppable even now in your later years. You have a strong, determined character that has taught me to pursue my dreams and aspirations in life. I have created this book in the hope that your love of food is shared with an even wider group of people. For me, Gran, your saying below sums up who you are and what I wish to share with others throughout my life:

"It is not how much you do, but how much love you put into the doing."

NATALIE OLDFIELD

CONTENTS

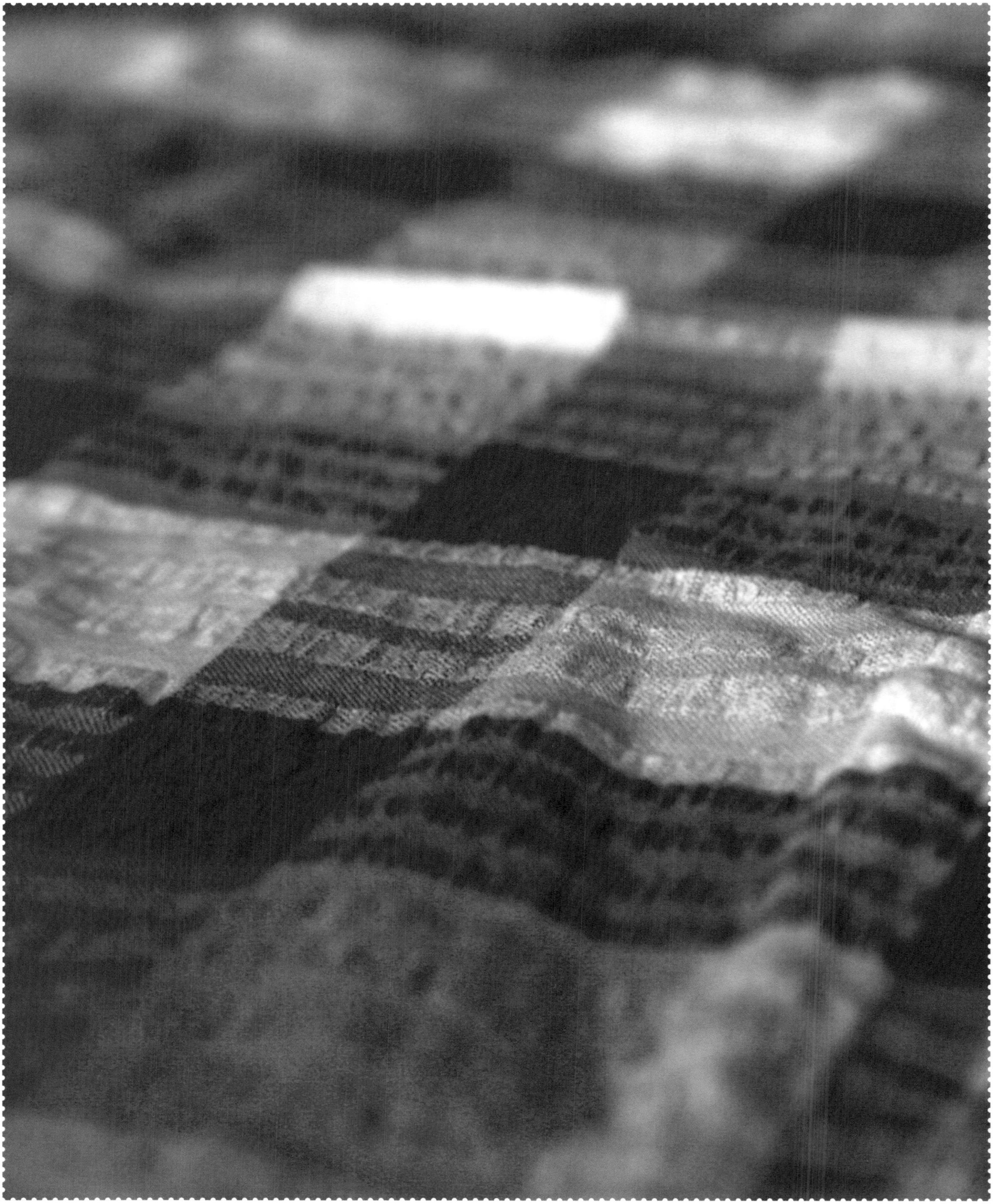

INTRODUCTION

I've dedicated this book to my Gran, Dulcie May Booker – but it is entirely her book anyway. Inspired by the love of food I inherited from her, and with her guidance, I have salvaged family favourite recipes from her cooking folders and notebooks. This resulting collection is meant as a tribute, and is also an attempt to capture a little bit of the enormous wealth of cooking and baking wisdom Gran has accumulated over her 95 years.

The words that immediately come to mind to describe Gran are "loving and hospitable". She welcomes family, friends and neighbours with home baking and a take-home pot of preserves, and, more importantly, by making us feel at home.

Together, her recipes tell the story of a busy community lifestyle, once common, now disappearing. Gran has lived all her life – nearly an entire century now – in Weymouth. She still lives in the house built for her and her husband Fred in 1942, a stone's throw away from the homestead where she grew up. . Weymouth is now a suburb of Manukau City, Auckland, but when Gran was born it was a rural community where her father and four uncles owned neighbouring farms. Gran and her three brothers grew up surrounded by paddocks full of cousins – she says the family "knew everyone in Weymouth from this end to the other".

I have a suspicion that's because in the early days, the family practically was everyone in Weymouth.

The kitchen was, and still is, the focal point – the heart – of her home. The cooking, as well as the eating, is a social activity she shares with those she loves. Gran is a great teacher and, when I was young, she would entice me into helping by explaining the "secret" of each particular recipe. Her warmth and enthusiasm – and being allowed to lick the bowl! – has always made cooking in her kitchen a very pleasurable experience.

Most of the recipes you'll find in this book are Gran's tried-and-true personal versions of much-loved New Zealand classics. Others are more modern – Gran can certainly move with the times.

Rediscovering some of our childhood treats for this book has been a delicious trip down memory lane for me and for my sister Michelle, who made and styled most of the food in this book. We discovered other recipes for the first time, which has been an equally mouth-watering history lesson. Here are the dishes which have traditionally filled the nation's tins and were spread on our tables, but which many of us have perhaps forgotten in recent years.

As Gran's notebooks are peppered with contributions from family and friends, so too have others contributed a few recipes to this book, including Flo, a particular friend of Gran's, whose shortbread is on page 67. As much as possible, we have faithfully copied the recipes just as they are written down in the notebooks. However, we have explained methods which are no longer standard, such as dredging and baking blind, and adapted recipes where necessary – modern ovens aren't heated by fire as

The importance of jam and cream in bonding a community should not be underestimated – Gran's life is testament to this.

some of Gran's recipes assume! Wherever ounces and pounds are mentioned, we have also given metric measurements; but we have left measurements in cups and tablespoons as they are. There is a conversion chart on page 184.

Most importantly, we are sharing not only Gran's recipes, but also the "secrets" which enticed me into her kitchen in the first place. The difference between average and extraordinary results can be as simple as beating well, or wiping the pan, or standing the custard. Small points, but effective.

Gran has achieved an enormous amount in a "quiet" life – as have many woman of her generation. I have immense admiration for who they are and what they do. Among other things, this book is a celebration of their way of life, a large part of which is the joy of sharing, of serving others and of creating love in the kitchen.

NATALIE OLDFIELD

Dulcie could cook by the time she was 10, and at age 12, she was so capable that she was entrusted with looking after the housekeeping and all the family meals while her mother was away for a fortnight. Everything, from bread to sponge cake to roast dinners, was made on the family's range, fueled by manuka wood found on their farm.

To check the oven was the right temperature, the cook would throw in some flour and see how long it took to go brown. Dulcie misses the range's manuka flavour: "Even the scones tasted different."

In the summer, perishables were put into a biscuit tin in a hole in the ground and covered with cold, wet sand. "We had a lot more work to do back then — it kept me out of mischief," says Dulcie. Substantial breakfasts full of protein helped to keep everyone's energy up.

BREAKFAST

EASY LITTLE BREAD

1 cup Plain Flour
1 cup Wholemeal Flour
1 cup Rolled Oats
1½ teaspoon Salt
1¼ cups Warm Water
2 teaspoons Dry Yeast
1 tablespoon Honey
Oil and Butter, for brushing

Mix flours, oats and salt together. Mix yeast into warm water until dissolved, then stir in honey. Pour wet mixture into flour, mix very well together.
Grease a loaf tin well with oil and butter. Turn dough into the tin and brush dough with oil or butter.
Cover with a damp cloth and leave in warm place for 30 minutes to rise. Leave in tin and bake for 35-40 minutes at 350°F (180°C).

"When I was growing up, you couldn't buy yeast at the store. We made our own from hops, sugar, potatoes and flour, and if we ran out, I would have to walk over the hill to my Aunty's, and get a bit of starter dough from her." - Dulcie

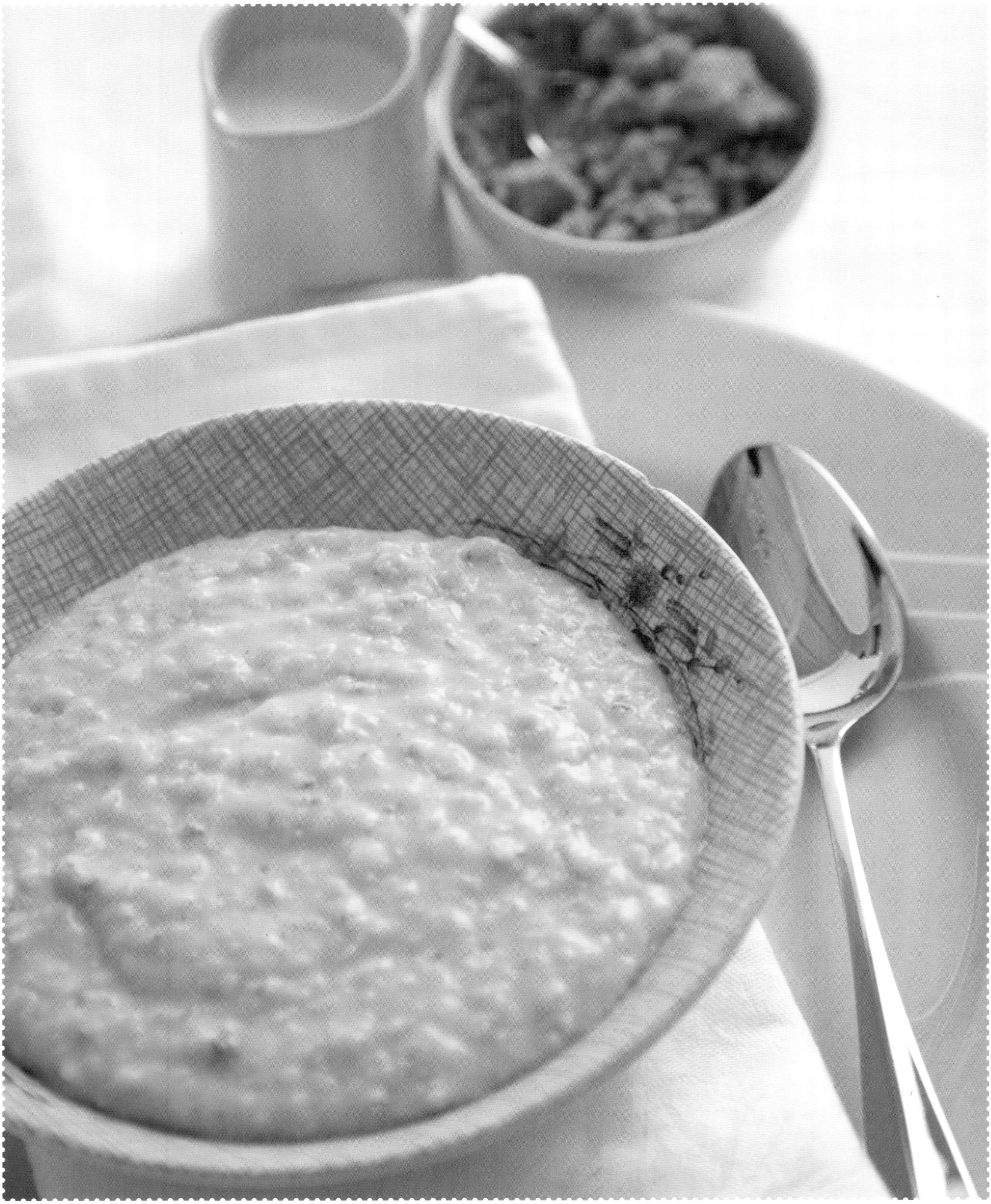

PORRIDGE

FOR A GENEROUS SERVING PER PERSON:
½ cup Rolled Oats
1½ cups Water
Salt to taste
Knob of Butter
Cream and Brown Sugar to serve

Soak rolled oats and salt in the water overnight.
Bring to boil and simmer for 3–5 minutes, depending on the
thickness desired. Stir occasionally. Add butter and stir until melted.
Serve with cream and brown sugar.

NATALIE'S MAPLE GRANOLA

2 cups Rolled Oats
5 cups Puffed Millet
1 cup Whole Almonds
½ cup Sunflower Seeds
½ cup Pumpkin Seeds
1 cup Flaked Coconut
1 cup Maple Syrup
½ cup Rice Bran Oil
½ cup Water
1 tablespoon Brown Sugar
½ teaspoon Cinnamon
1 teaspoon Vanilla Essence
½ teaspoon Salt
1 teaspoon Nutmeg

"This recipe was inspired by a visit to New York. I like to use organic ingredients as it makes a big difference to the taste." - Natalie

In a bowl mix together the oats, puffed millet, almonds, seeds and flaked coconut. Put the rice bran oil, maple syrup, water, sugar, vanilla essence, cinnamon, nutmeg and salt in a saucepan. Bring just to a boil, stirring constantly, then pour over the dry ingredients. Mix well. There should be no excess liquid at the bottom of the pan and the mixture should be sticky — if the mixture is too wet add more oats. Spread out evenly on a baking tray and bake for 1 hour at 325°F (160°C). Reduce the temperature to 275°F (140°C) and continue cooking for another hour. Switch off the oven and leave to dry out for at least a further hour, and overnight if possible.

GRANDMA ETTEMA'S BANANA NUT BREAD

1½ cups White Sugar
½ cup Shortening (Crisco)
2 Eggs, beaten
3 Ripe Bananas, mashed
2 teaspoons Baking Soda
⅔ cup Milk
½ cup Walnuts, chopped
½ teaspoon Salt
1 teaspoon Vanilla
3 cups Flour

Cream shortening and sugar together. Add beaten eggs and mashed bananas. Warm milk and add baking soda, stand a few minutes and then add to the banana mix. Mix in flour, salt, vanilla and nuts. Pour into five tin cans, filling each just over halfway (any more and they will overflow during baking).
Let stand for 10 minutes before baking.
Bake at 350°F (180°C) for 50 minutes.
Remove from oven and turn out onto a cooling rack. Cover with a light towel so they don't dry out.

Cakes can also be baked in tin cans – cook them at the temperature suggested by the recipe, but for a shorter length of time.

MUSHROOMS ON TOAST

2 cups Field Mushrooms
2 tablespoons Butter
Salt and Pepper

Peel mushrooms and slice. Heat butter in pan until hot. Add mushrooms and cook for 5–8 minutes, then add salt and pepper to taste.

Serve with Easy Little Bread (recipe page 16).

"I sent the boys out to pick fresh mushrooms from the farm in the mornings and we ate them immediately for breakfast." - Dulcie

BOOKERS' MESS

2 Tomatoes, peeled and quartered
Salt and Pepper
Knob of Butter
3 Eggs, beaten
Parsley to serve

Dry chopped tomatoes on paper towels. Sprinkle with salt and
pepper. Heat butter in pan, add tomatoes, fry for 30 seconds or until
just heated. Stir in eggs and scramble gently until cooked.
Serve with chopped parsley.

*To make it easier to peel the tomatoes, cover them with boiling
water, drain and then rinse with cold water. Peel with a small knife.*

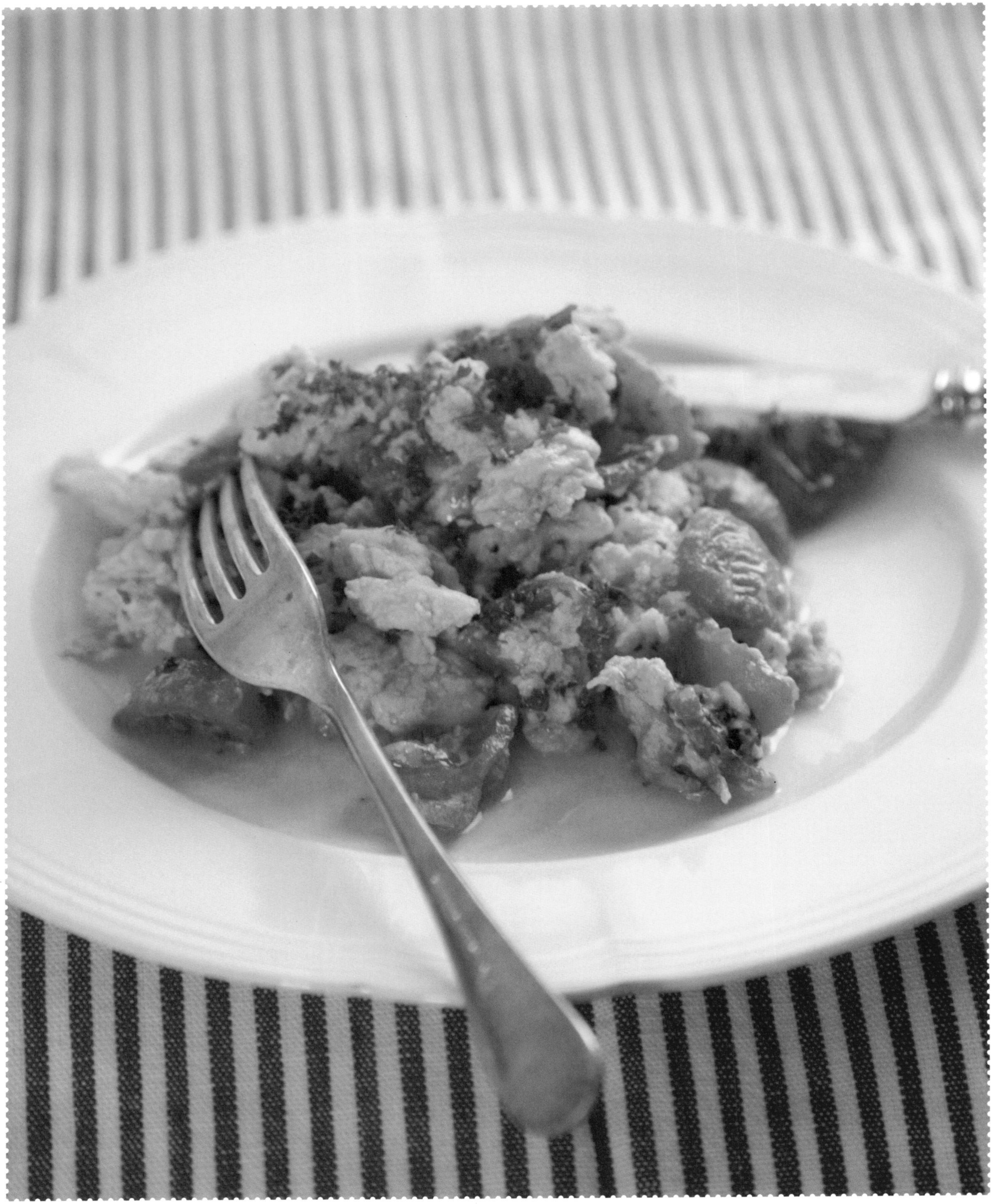

SUNDAY ROAST FRY-UP

6 Streaky Bacon Rashers
1 cup Leftover Roasted Vegetables
¼ cup Leftover Greens
Oil for frying
Salt and Pepper

Heat oil in pan and add bacon. Cook until crispy.
Add roasted vegetables and greens and fry until hot.
Add salt and pepper to taste.

Serve with homemade Tomato Sauce (recipe page 167).

"On Sundays, we'd put the meat on for the roast before we went to church in the morning, and the veges on when we came back. Mum used to say 'now dear, make sure you do enough veges for tomorrow's fry-up'." - Dulcie

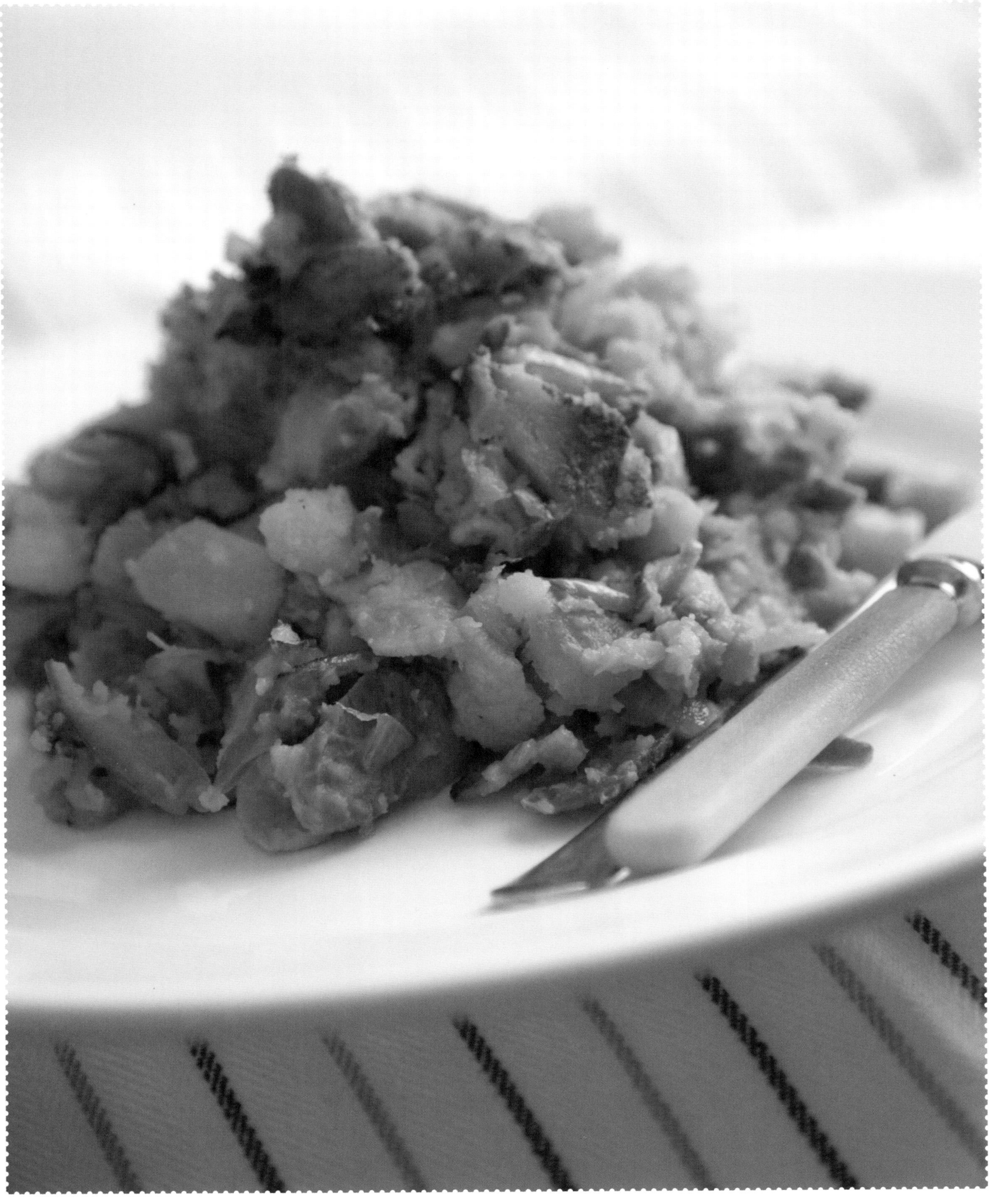

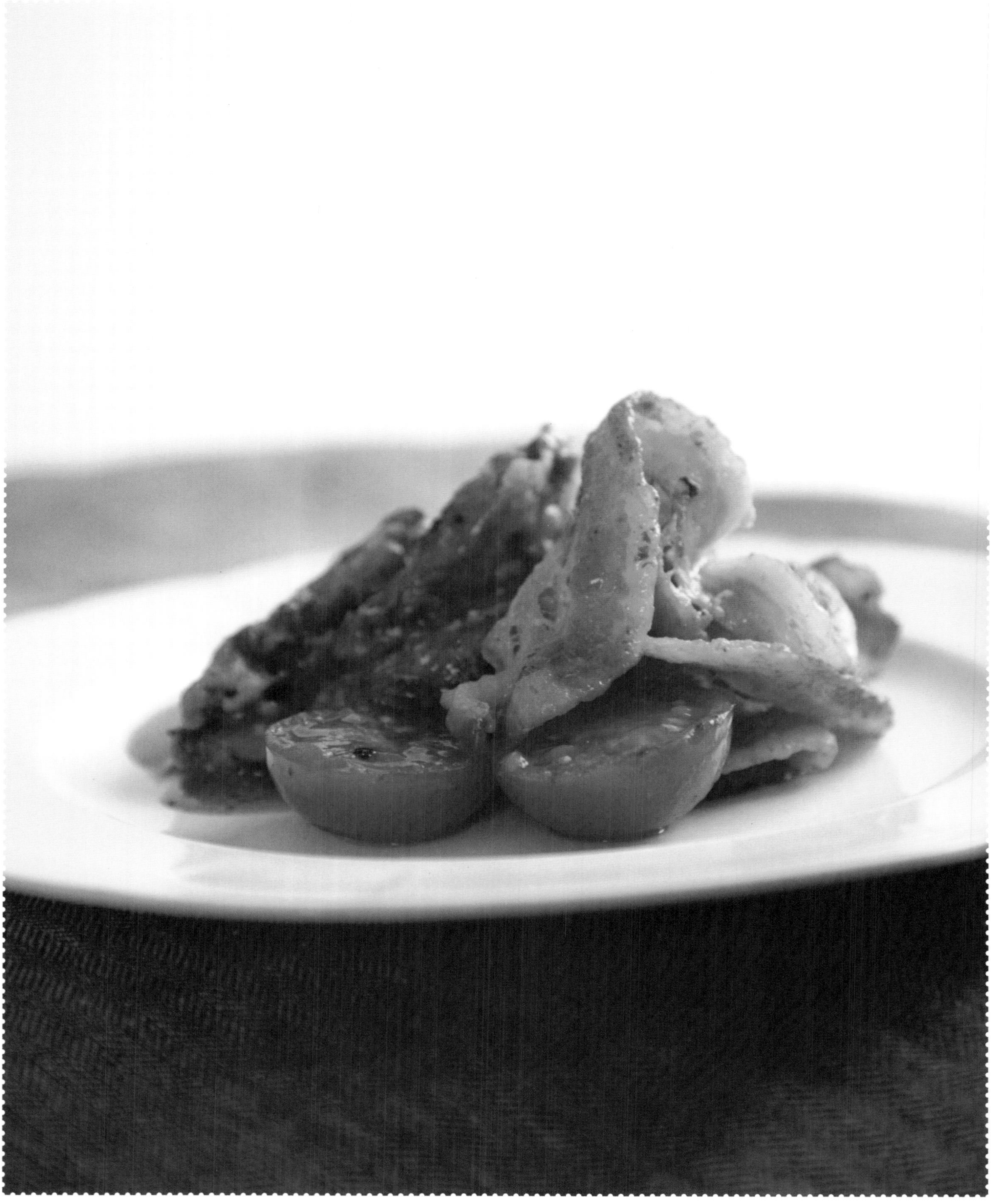

LAMB'S FRY AND BACON

100g Lamb's Fry
Milk
¼ cup Flour
Pinch Salt
6 Streaky Bacon Rashers

Slice lamb's fry into half inch (1.25cm) slices. Flip it in milk, and
then cover in flour and salt. Fry bacon and take out of pan. Using
the fat left in the pan from the bacon, cook the lamb's fry, 3 minutes
each side.
Make gravy by gradually adding a little flour and water to the juices
from lamb's fry left in the pan.

**"I would give this to the children at least once
a week, as liver is good for the blood." – Dulcie**

FLOURED FLOUNDER

2 Fresh Flounder
½ cup Flour
¼ cup Milk
Salt and Pepper to taste
Oil for frying

Wash and dry flounder. Pour milk onto plate. Mix flour, salt and
pepper on another plate. Cover flounder with milk and then with
flour mixture.
Cook on hot pan for 4 minutes on each side or until golden brown.

This recipe also works well for snapper, kahawai and trevelly.

**"Fred would rise in the middle of the night
to go fishing, and in the morning the family
would sometimes wake up to fresh flounder
he'd left on the bench, ready for a breakfast
feast." - Dulcie**

12   TUESDAY, JULY 17, 1984

Weymouth CWI celebrate golden jubilee

"Without the Women's Institute, the Village would be destitute."

That quote was found in an autograph book belonging to the Weymouth Country Women's Institute, written by Mrs O. Bilgham on April 25, 1939.

Last Wednesday, July 11, about 150 members of the Weymouth CWI gathered at the Weymouth Hall to celebrate their branch's golden jubilee.

When the Weymouth Hall was destroyed by fire in 1982, scattered records and remains of the CWI were found and compiled into a shore history by Mrs B. L.

August 1, with an attendance of 21 members. Monthly meetings followed with regular good attendances and the first social, to raise funds for crockery, was held on November 24, 1934.

In June 1936 it was proposed to write to the branch's counterpart in Weymouth, England, and many interesting letters have been exchanged over the years since.

Around this time many of the meetings were held in the homes or gardens of members, because of a lack of facilities in the hall. Because of this lack of facilities, according to minutes of May 1938, the secretary was instructed

meetings.

In February 1944, the president asked members to discuss the future of the institute and examine the possibility of either going into recess or closing down altogether. The members decided to meet every second month.

For several years they struggled on with as few as two to ten members attending meetings, but gradually membership increased and monthly meetings resumed.

Today the Weymouth branch of the Country Women's Institute has over 50 members with more joining all the time

Weymouth Country Women's Institute

Golden Jubilee

1934 - 1984

Dulcie was a member of the Weymouth Women's Institute from the time she was 18. The women would meet monthly to hear an outside expert speak about topics such as cooking and cross-stitch. Dulcie's cheese straws always went down a treat.

The highlight of the year was the Institute competition for baking, preserves, floral arrangement and so on. The items to be judged changed annually – one year they might include pikelets, the next, scones. Dulcie was known for her kisses – the baked kind that is! One judge said they were perfect. Her scones usually came first too. According to one of Dulcie's rivals, "it's no use making scones when Dulcie does, because we know hers are the best!"

Institute judges weren't the only group to appreciate Dulcie's baking talents. "Oh, you had to fill up the tins if you had brothers," says Dulcie. "I once filled a big tin to the brim with melting moments. All it took was a neighbourhood cricket match – and the biscuits all disappeared!"

MORNING TEA

GINGER LIME LOAF

LOAF
250g Butter
½ cup Brown Sugar
⅔ cup Golden Syrup
2 tablespoons Fresh Ginger, finely grated
1 tablespoon Lime Rind
1 cup Flour
1 cup Self-Raising Flour
2 Eggs, lightly beaten
¾ cup Plain Yoghurt

LIME ICING
2 cups Icing Sugar
¼ teaspoon Butter, melted
2 tablespoons Lime Juice
¼ teaspoon Lime Rind

For the loaf: melt butter and golden syrup, add sugar, ginger, and lime. Stir over low heat until sugar is dissolved. Sift flours together. In a separate bowl, mix eggs and yoghurt.
Add both liquid mixtures to the flour alternately; be careful not to over-beat the mixture.
Pour into tin and bake for 50 minutes at 350°F (180°C).
For the icing: mix together sifted icing sugar and butter, lime juice and rind and spread over cool loaf.

"Gran has continued to update her baking — this is a favourite she has discovered in recent years." - Natalie

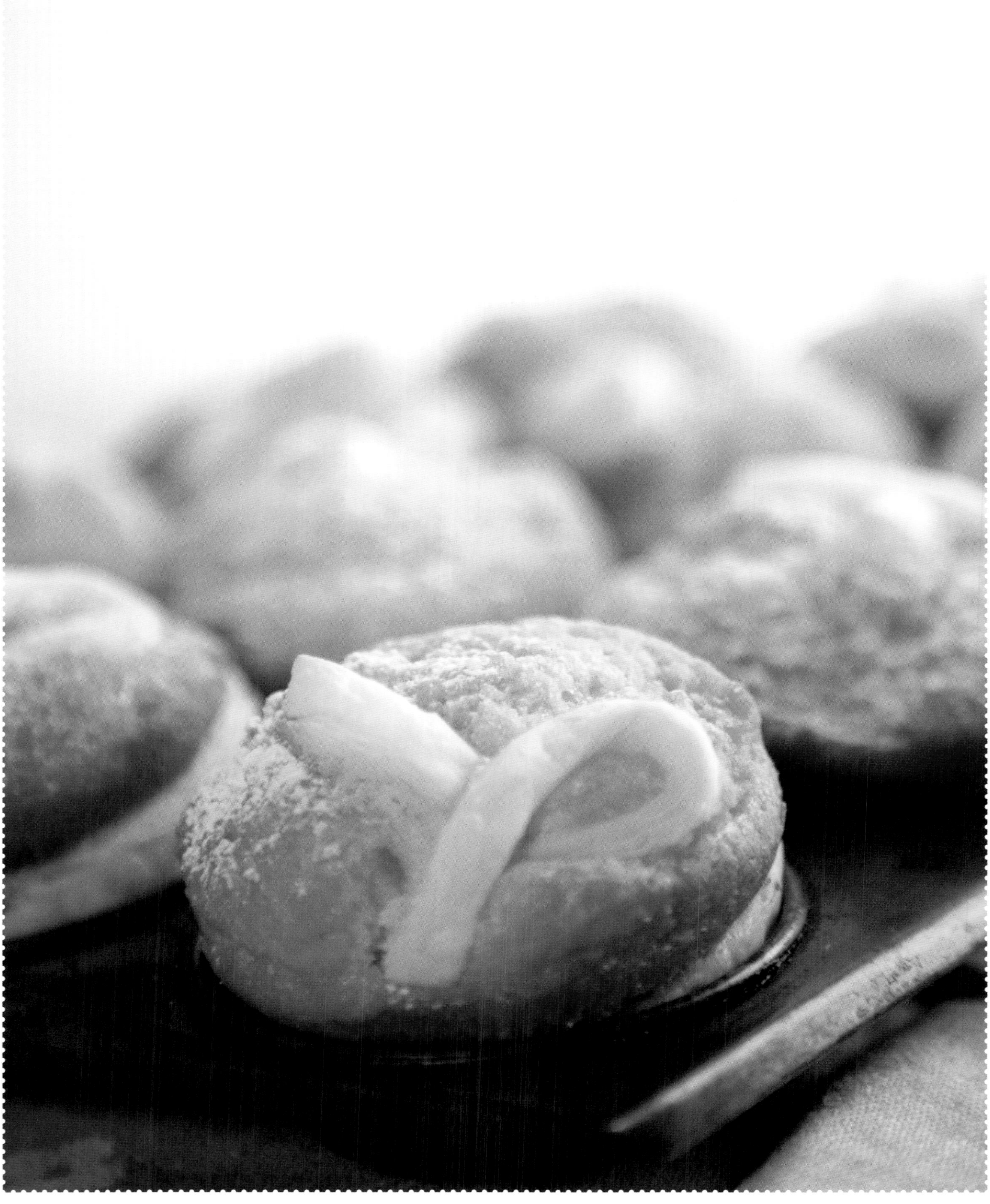

CHEESE CAKES

2 - 3 Sheets Flaky Pastry
Raspberry Jam
4 oz (115g) Butter
4 oz (115g) Sugar
2 Eggs
5 oz (140g) Flour
1 teaspoon Baking Powder

Line about 20 patty tins with pastry. Put a teaspoon of jam at the bottom of each.
Mix together butter and sugar until light and fluffy, then add eggs one at a time, beating well after each addition. Fold in sifted flour and baking powder until combined.
Put a large spoonful of cake mixture on the top of jam. Place a small piece of crossed pastry on the top of cake mixture.
Bake about 20 minutes at 400°F (200°C).

"These are favourites of mine. Don't be stingy with the jam, but put it in the centre so it doesn't creep up the sides. Dust with a wee bit of icing sugar when they're cooked, but don't be too heavy-handed about it." - Dulcie

NAPOLEONS

3 - 4 Sheets Puff Pastry
2 cups Icing Sugar
2 tablespoons Butter, softened
Boiling Water
Raspberry Essence to taste
Raspberry Jam
300ml Cream, whipped

Cut pastry into rectangles, a little larger than desired size as they shrink during cooking (roughly 8cm x 15cm).
Place on greased oven tray and bake at 400°F (200°C) for 10 minutes. Set aside to cool.
Sift icing sugar into bowl and add butter. Cream mixture while slowly adding boiling water to a spreadable consistency. Stir in raspberry essence.
Spread bottoms with jam then whipped cream, and spread the tops with icing.
Sandwich tops and bottoms together.

SAUSAGE ROLLS

250g Premium Beef Mince
250g Sausage Meat
1 Onion, finely chopped
Boiling Water
Flour
4 Sheets Flaky Pastry
Milk for brushing

Mix sausage meat and mince together. Pour boiling water over onion, drain immediately and mix into meat.

Shape meat mixture into rolls the length of the pastry sheets, and roll them in flour. Place each pastry sheet separately on flat surface and wet one edge of the pastry so that the meat will stick to it. Then place meat on the damp area and roll up the pastry sheet to form a log. Cut into desired size and brush each sausage roll with milk.

Cook at 400°F (200°C) for approximately 20 minutes, or until golden brown and cooked thoroughly.

MELTING MOMENTS

BISCUITS
1 tablespoon Icing Sugar
¼ lb (110g) Flour
¼ lb (115g) Butter, softened

ICING
1½ cups Icing Sugar
3 tablespoons Butter, softened
1 Passionfruit
Water

For the biscuits: sift icing sugar and flour together. Add butter to dry ingredients and mix well. Spoon in small quantities onto greased oven tray, or onto baking paper on tray.
Bake at 350°F (180°C) for 15 minutes.
For the icing: sift icing sugar and add butter and pulp of passionfruit. Mix to combine, adding water until still firm but spreadable.
Spread between cooked biscuits and dust with icing sugar.

CREAM CRACKERS

1 lb (455g) Flour
½ teaspoon Salt
3 oz (85g) Butter
Milk to mix

Sift the flour and salt, rub in butter and mix in milk to make a stiff
dough. Roll out thinly. Cut in squares, place on greased oven tray
and prick with a fork.
Bake in quick oven (400°F, 200°C) until golden brown
(approximately 10 minutes).

"These are an everyday staple. I love having lots
of people in the house — and every one of my
visitors gets cream crackers topped with cheese
and tomato to go with their cup of tea." - Dulcie

CHEESE STRAWS

2 Sheets Flaky or Puff Pastry
1 cup of Tasty Cheese, finely grated
Cayenne Pepper to taste
1 Egg, beaten

Roll out each sheet of pastry separately, until very thin. Sprinkle with cheese and cayenne pepper.
Fold each sheet into three. Roll out again, not too thinly this time. Brush with beaten egg. Cut either length ways or crossways to desired width and twist.
Place on greased tray and bake at 400°F (200°C) for 15-20 minutes.

PIKELETS

2 cups Flour
Pinch Salt
½ cup Caster Sugar
3 Eggs
4 tablespoons Butter, melted
½ teaspoon Vanilla Essence
1 cup Milk
2 heaped teaspoons Baking Powder
Butter, or Cream and Jam, to serve

Sift flour, salt and sugar into a bowl. Make a well and drop in the
eggs, melted butter and vanilla essence. Add milk slowly, mixing
to a smooth but not sloppy consistency. Once mixed, stir in baking
powder with fork.
Place tablespoonfuls into hot buttered pan, turning them when
bubbles appear.
Make sure you wipe the pan with a cloth or paper towel after each
lot of pikelets is cooked.
Serve with butter or cream and jam.

*Use a heavy pan, preferably cast iron. Wiping the pan between each
batch takes away any dirty burnt butter, keeping the pikelets golden.*

ANZAC BISCUITS

1 cup Flour
1 cup Sugar
1 cup Rolled Oats
Pinch Salt
1 cup Coconut
1 cup Walnuts, chopped
¼ lb (115g) Butter
1 tablespoon Golden Syrup
1 teaspoon Baking Soda
1 tablespoon Boiling Water

Mix all dry ingredients in a bowl.
Melt butter and golden syrup, then add baking soda dissolved in
water. Mix wet into dry ingredients.
Spoon onto greased oven tray and bake at 320°F (160°C) for
15 minutes.

GINGERBREAD

1 cup Sugar
1 cup Butter
4 Eggs
1 cup Golden Syrup
3 cups Flour
1 tablespoon Ginger
1 teaspoon Cinnamon
1 dessertspoon Baking Soda
1 cup Boiling Water

Cream butter and sugar, add eggs and golden syrup, and then sifted dry ingredients. Dissolve soda in water and add to mixture.
Bake for 1½ to 2 hours at 320°F (160°C).

"Grandad made the gingerbread tin pictured opposite from wartime biscuit tins. It is particularly thin, which we found helps in the baking process." - Natalie

CREAM PUFFS

1 cup Water
3 oz (85g) Butter
5 oz (140g) Flour
1 tablespoon Sugar
½ teaspoon Vanilla Essence
4 Eggs
Whipped Cream, for filling
Icing Sugar to serve

Bring butter and water to the boil. Add flour and beat until the mixture leaves the sides of the saucepan. Remove from heat, then add sugar and vanilla essence. Add eggs one at a time and beat well after each addition. Place spoonfuls onto a greased oven tray and bake at 400°F (200°C) for 30 minutes.
When the puffs are cold, split and fill them with fresh cream and dust with icing sugar.

The secret is – beat well. For a modern take on this traditional favourite, drizzle with melted chocolate.

PARTY CHEESE SCONES

TOPPING
2 tablespoons Butter, melted
3 tablespoons Cheese, finely grated
Pinch Dry Mustard
Pinch Cayenne Pepper
1 Egg

SCONES
2 cups Flour
4 teaspoons Baking Powder
50g Butter
½ cup Cheese, grated
¾ cup Milk

For the topping: combine melted butter, mustard, cayenne pepper and cheese. Beat egg and add to cheese mixture. Set aside while preparing scones.
For the scones: sift flour and baking powder, cut in butter to resemble breadcrumbs. Add cheese. Stir in enough milk to make stiff dough. Place dough on floured surface and gently press out into a slab about 1 inch (3cm) thick. Spoon topping mixture over the dough, and cut into 18 small rounds.
Bake at 430°F (220°C) for 12 minutes.

"The extra effort to mix the glaze is well worth it." - Dulcie

STRAWBERRY SLICE

1 packet Strawberry Jelly
1 cup Self-Raising Flour
½ cup Caster Sugar
60g Butter
1 Egg
500g Fresh Strawberries, sliced

Dissolve jelly as per packet instructions, and set aside to cool. Sift flour into bowl, add sugar and mix well. Rub in butter and add egg to form a dough.

Press dough into slice tin and bake at 350°F (180°C) for 20 minutes. When the base is cool, place sliced strawberries on top and pour over cooled jelly. Place in fridge until jelly has set.

MADELINES

½ packet Jelly Crystals
¾ cup Hot Water
2 oz (55g) Butter
2 oz (55g) Sugar
1 Egg
2 oz (55g) Flour
1 teaspoon Baking Powder
1 tablespoon Milk
Coconut

Dissolve jelly crystals into hot water, set aside to cool.
Cream butter and sugar, drop in egg and beat well. Fold in sifted
flour and baking powder, then add milk. Mix until just combined.
Bake in 6 small greased moulds for 20 minutes at 400°F (200°C).
Turn out, brush with cool jelly, and sprinkle with coconut.

**"Gran's madelines are not French 'madeleines',
but delicious jelly versions of the English jam
madeline." - Natalie**

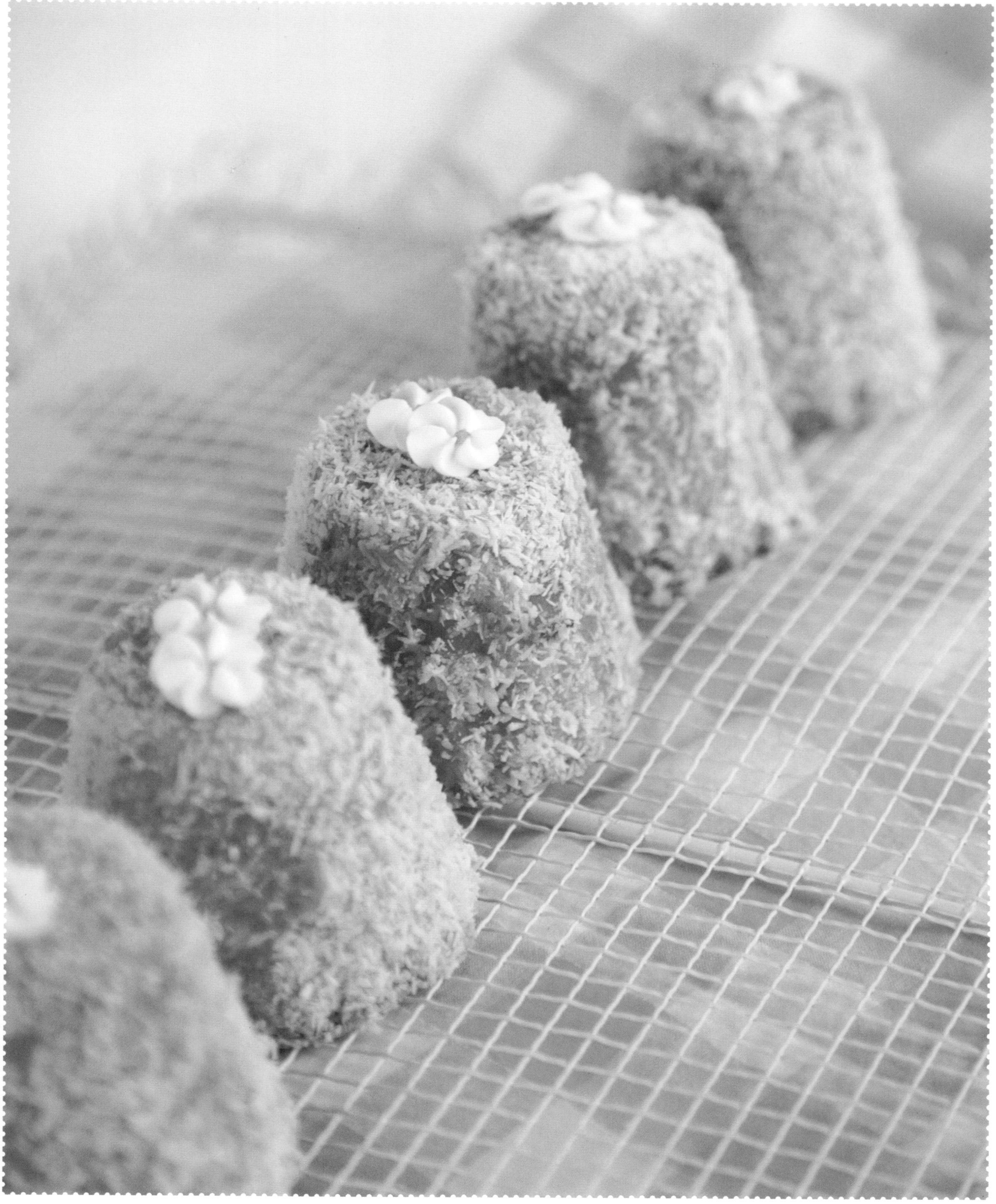

FLO'S SHORTBREAD

½ lb (225g) Butter (room temperature)
1 cup Icing Sugar
1½ cups Cornflour
1 cup Flour
Pinch Salt

Beat butter and icing sugar together with electric beater until smooth. Fold in sifted flours and salt until combined. Roll into a log, then sit it in fridge for no more than 10 minutes. Cut into rounds. Place rounds onto greased oven tray and bake at 300°F (150°C) for 30 minutes.

HONEY GEMS

2 tablespoons Honey
1 tablespoon Sugar
2 tablespoons Butter
1 Egg
½ cup Milk
1 cup Flour
1 teaspoon Baking Powder
¼ teaspoon Soda

Cream butter, sugar and honey. Add egg and give mixture a beating.
Add other ingredients, and beat the mixture well.
Half fill greased gem irons. Bake at 350°F (180°C) for 10–15 minutes.

**"Honey is one of my favourite flavours —
especially the wild honey we ate as children.
Dad collected it from the wild bees who built
their hives on our farm." – Dulcie**

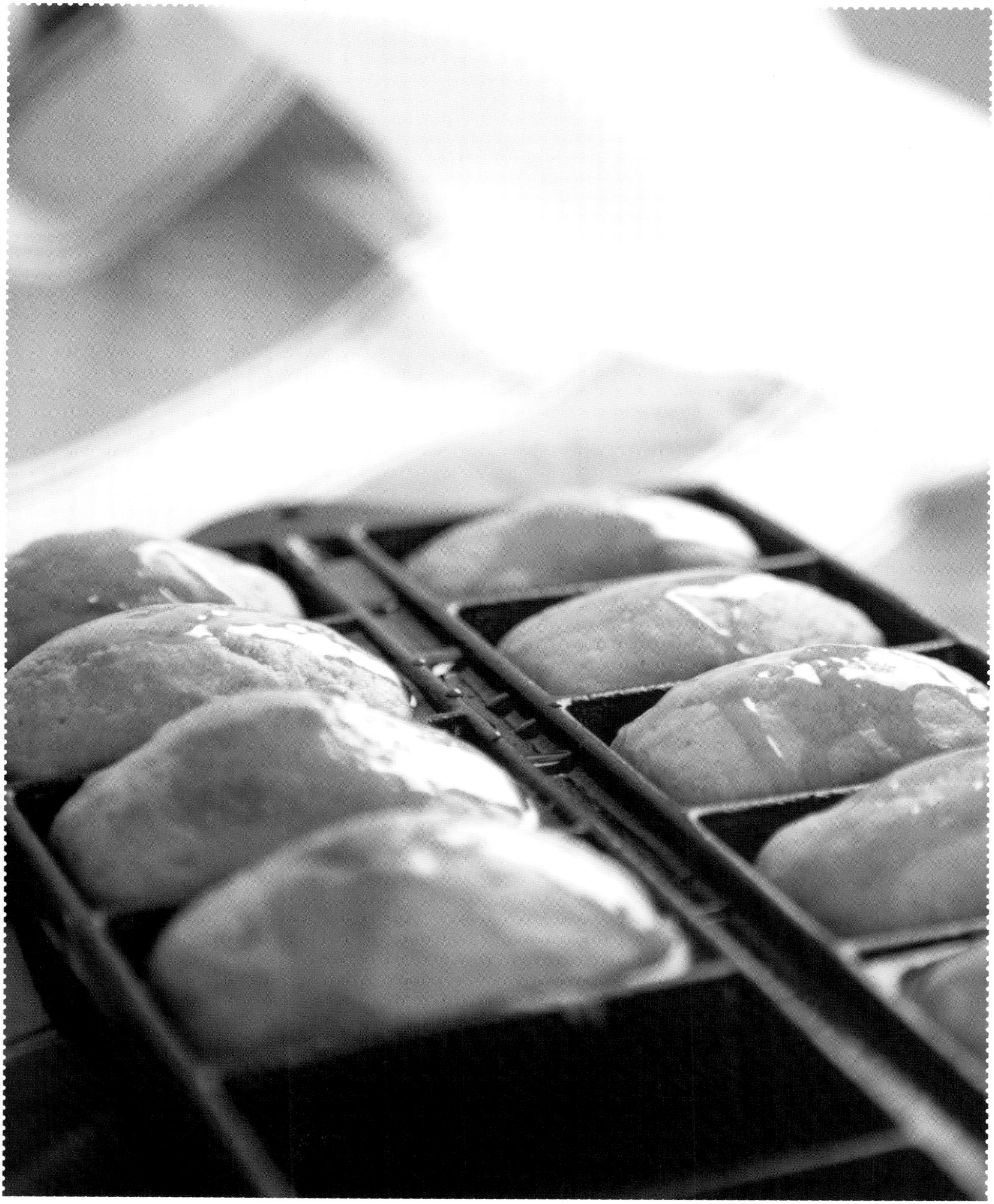

KISSES

6 oz (170g) Butter
6 oz (170g) Sugar
3 Eggs
6 oz (170g) Flour
6 oz (170g) Cornflour
1½ teaspoons Baking Powder
Raspberry Jam
Icing Sugar

Cream butter and sugar well, adding eggs one at a time. Add twice-sifted flours and baking powder. Put small, even spoonfuls onto greased baking trays.
Bake 8-10 minutes at 400°F (200°C). When they're cold, sandwich pairs together with raspberry jam, and sprinkle with icing sugar.

"Would you like a kiss, dear?" – Dulcie

APPLE SHORTCAKE

2½ cups Self-Raising Flour
1½ cups Sugar
190g Butter
2 Eggs, lightly beaten
2 cups Apples, peeled, sliced and cooked
Milk, for brushing

Sift flour into a bowl, add sugar and stir to combine. Rub in butter
and then add egg to form soft dough. Press half the dough into a
greased slice tin, cover with cooked apple. Roll out the rest of the
dough and place on top of apple. Brush over with milk.
Bake 20-30 minutes at 350°F (180°C). Sprinkle with icing sugar and
slice while hot.

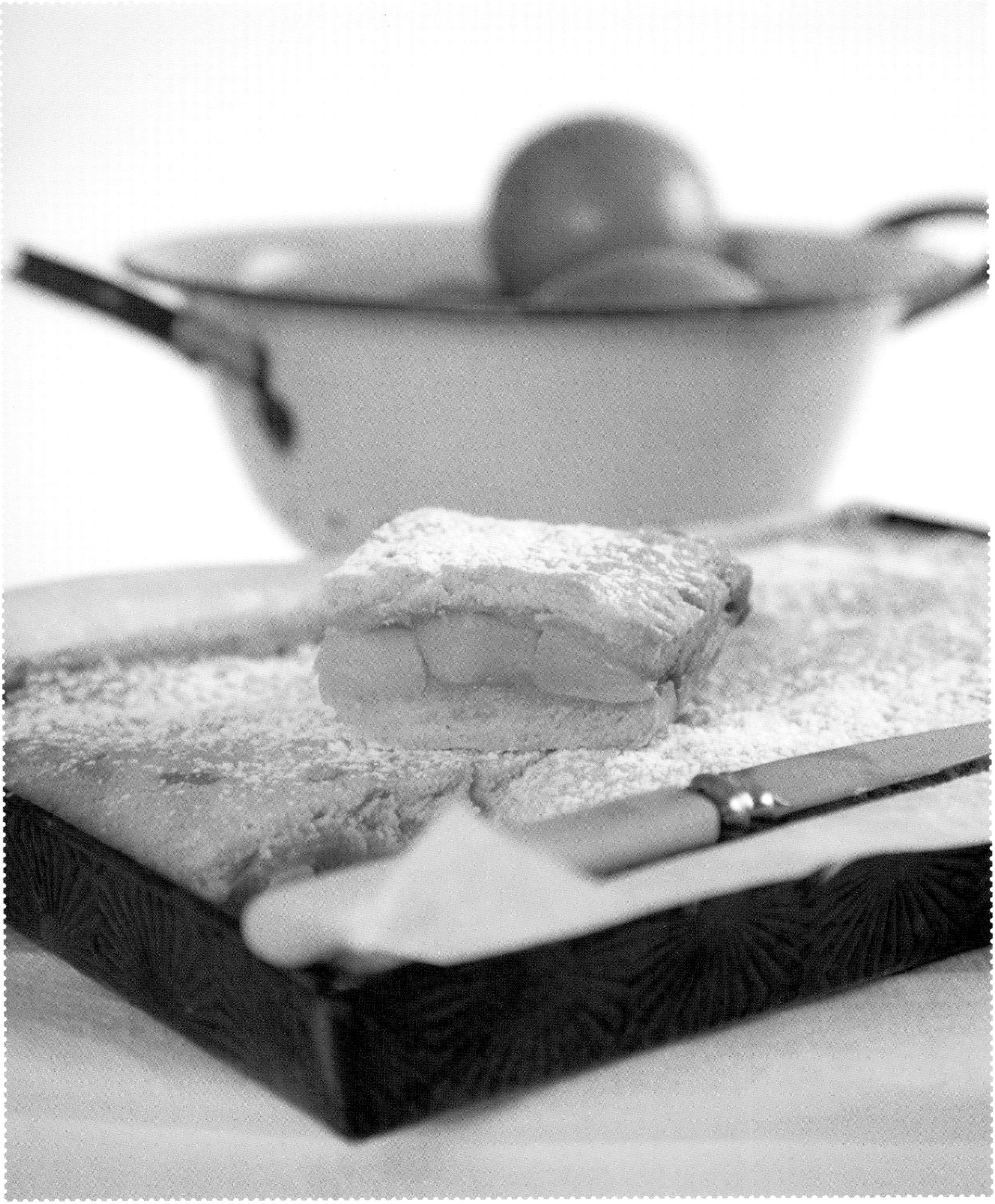

LOUISE CAKE

CAKE
5 oz (140g) Butter
2 oz (55g) Sugar
2 Egg Yolks
10 oz (280g) Flour
2 teaspoons Baking Powder
½ cup Strawberry or Raspberry Jam

MERINGUE
4 oz (115g) Sugar
2 Egg Whites
4 oz (115g) Coconut

For the cake: cream butter and sugar, then add egg yolks and beat well. Stir in sifted flour and baking powder. Press mixture into greased tray. Spread jam over mixture.
For the meringue: beat egg whites and sugar together until thick, then fold in coconut.
Spread the meringue on top of cake.
Bake at 350°F (180°C) for 30 minutes. Cut into squares.

MARSHMALLOWS

1½ cups Caster Sugar
⅔ cup Hot Water
2 tablespoons Gelatine
½ cup Cold Water
1 teaspoon Vanilla Essence
Red Food Colouring
Cornflour for dusting

Grease 16.5cm x 26cm pan. Line with baking paper, allowing a 3cm overhang at both ends.
Combine sugar and hot water in saucepan, stir over medium heat for about 3 minutes or until sugar is dissolved. Using a fork, combine gelatine with cold water. Pour into hot sugar syrup and stir on medium heat until the mixture is clear and gelatine is dissolved.
Pour into electric mixer bowl and set aside to cool (about 40 minutes).
Using mixer, beat until very thick. Add vanilla and colouring, beat for another minute.
Spread into pan and smooth the top. Set aside at room temperature for approximately 1 hour.
Lift onto board, and cut into squares using a wet knife.
Lightly dust with cornflour.

Spread the marshmallow on a cooked shortcake base (recipe page 87) to make marshmallow slice.

PEANUT BROWNIES

250g Butter
2 cups Sugar
2 Eggs
2 teaspoons Vanilla Essence
2 cups Flour
2 tablespoons Cocoa
½ teaspoon Salt
1 teaspoon Baking Powder
2½ cups Roasted Peanuts
1 cup Coconut

Cream butter and sugar well, add eggs one at a time, beat well then add vanilla essence. Sift flour, baking powder, cocoa and salt into creamed mixture, and then fold in coconut and roasted peanuts. Drop dessertspoons onto cold greased tray.
Bake at 340°F (170°C) for 20-25 minutes.

Don't cook the brownies too fast because they're easily burnt. To roast your own peanuts, put them on a baking dish in a low heat oven for 20 minutes, shaking them occasionally. You can keep their skins on – they're not too husky for this recipe.

"These peanut brownies have been a special 'Granny present' for family and friends on many occasions." – Natalie

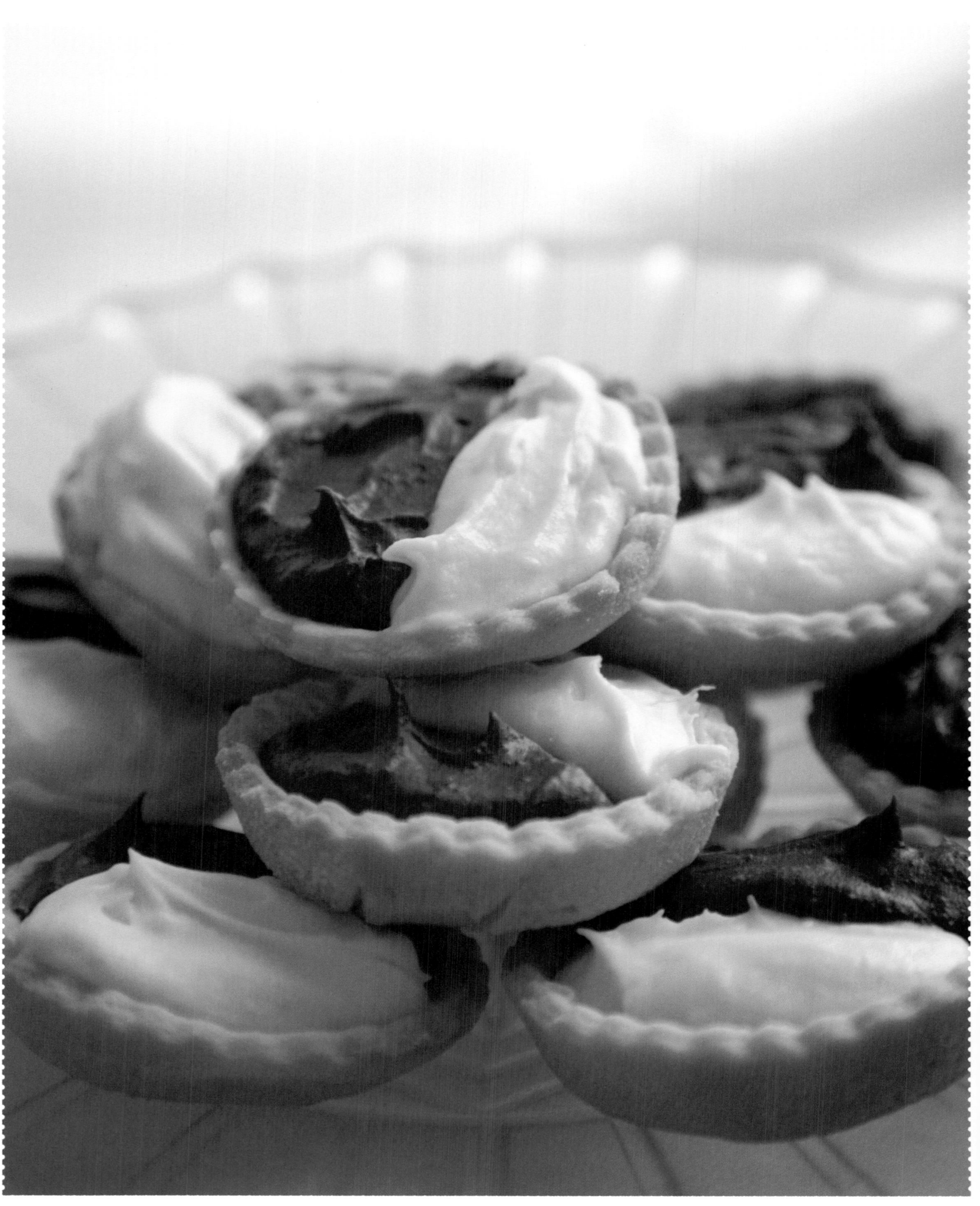

NEENISH TARTS

PASTRY
4 oz (115g) Butter
4 oz (115g) Sugar
1 Egg
8 oz (225g) Flour
1 teaspoon Baking Powder
Pinch Salt

FILLING
4 tablespoons Butter
8 tablespoons Icing Sugar
4 tablespoons Sweetened Condensed Milk
2 dessertspoons Lemon Juice
2 tablespoons Cocoa

For the pastry: cream butter and sugar, add egg and beat well. Sift
dry ingredients and mix with creamed mixture. Knead well. Roll out
and cut into rounds.
Grease patty tins and line with pastry rounds. Prick pastry with a
fork and bake at 350°F (180°C) for about 10 minutes.
For the filling: soften butter, add sifted icing sugar, condensed milk
and lemon juice. Divide mixture in half and add cocoa to half the
mixture. Mix to combine. Make sure both mixtures are the same
consistency — you may need to add a little more icing sugar to the
white mixture.
Place a spoonful of each mixture side by side into each of the pastry
cases. Put in fridge to set.

COCONUT ICE

3 cups Sugar
1 cup Glucose Powder
1 teaspoon Butter
¼ teaspoon Cream of Tartar
1 cup Milk
Pinch Salt
1 cup Coconut
Vanilla Essence
Red Food Colouring

Mix together sugar, glucose powder, butter, cream of tartar, milk and
salt in a pan.
Bring slowly to the boil, then boil for 10 minutes, stirring continuously.
Take off heat and beat in coconut and a few drops of vanilla essence.
Stand pan in cold water and beat until it thickens.
Pour half into buttered slice tin, then beat the food colouring into
the other half, before pouring it on top of the uncoloured mix.
Leave to set in fridge. Cut when set.

GRANNY BARR'S RAISIN SCROLLS

4 cups Flour
2 teaspoons Baking Powder
1 teaspoon Salt
175g Butter
1 cup Milk
Melted Butter for spreading
1 cup Raisins
1 cup Brown Sugar
1 teaspoon Cinnamon

Sift flour, baking powder and salt. Rub in butter, add milk to make
a dough.
Roll out the dough and spread lightly with melted butter and
sprinkle with cinnamon, sugar and raisins. Roll up and cut into
1½ inch (4cm) pieces. Place scrolls on tray.
Bake 20 minutes at 400°F (200°C).

"This is MY Gran's recipe!" - Dulcie

LUSCIOUS LEMON SLICE

BASE
1 cup Self-Raising Flour
½ cup Caster Sugar
60g Butter
1 Egg, lightly beaten

FILLING
¼ cup Lemon Juice
½ cup Caster Sugar
1 Egg, lightly beaten
60g Butter

For the base: sift flour into bowl, add sugar, stir well to combine.
Rub in butter and add egg to form soft dough.
Press two thirds into tin.
For the filling: place all filling ingredients into small pot and cook over low heat till thick.
Pour the hot filling over the dough in tin. Crumb remaining dough over top.
Bake at 350°F (180°C) for 30 minutes.

"Lemons are easy to use, as the tree is just outside the back door. I love them; I eat them like oranges." – Dulcie

In the 1930s, when Dulcie was in her early twenties, her brother Alan ran fortnightly dances at Weymouth Hall. Young people would come from as far away as Onehunga, 12 miles up the road, to foxtrot and two-step to accordion and piano music. The boys would decorate the hall with ferns; the girls would set their hair and make their own evening gowns — "no boosies showing," remembers Dulcie. A favourite gown of hers was pale green crepe with organza pink roses sewn just above the knee.

Of course, one of the highlights of the evening would be the supper. Most of the ladies didn't have to bring "a plate" because Alan provided the supper — or rather, his sister and cousins did. Alan made sure his girls concocted good, substantial sandwiches of salmon, lettuce, egg and tomato — "none of these half-filled things," he instructed. And they would bring masses of dainties, like kisses and cream puffs, as well as several cakes — often sponges and madeira cake.

CAKES

PASSIONFRUIT SPONGE CAKE

CAKE
¾ cup Sugar
4 Eggs
1 cup Flour
½ teaspoon Baking Powder
1 large tablespoon Butter
2 large tablespoons Boiling Water

ICING
1½ cups Icing Sugar, sifted
4 tablespoons Butter, softened
2 Passionfruit
Pouring Cream to mix (approx ¼ cup)

Whipped Cream to fill sponge

For the cake: Beat sugar and eggs very well. Fold in flour and baking powder then melted butter and lastly water.
Bake at 320°F (160°C) for 20 minutes.
For the icing: place icing sugar, butter and passionfruit pulp in mixing bowl. Mix well, adding cream to make it really light and creamy. Once cake has cooled, cut sponge in half and fill with whipped cream, then spread icing on top.

NATALIE'S MOIST CHOCOLATE CAKE

CAKE
100g Butter
2 tablespoons Golden Syrup
2 Eggs
1 tablespoon Vanilla Essence
2 cups Sugar
2 cups Self-Raising Flour
½ cup Cocoa
2 cups Warm Milk
2 teaspoons Baking Soda

ICING
1½ cups Icing Sugar
2 tablespoons Butter
2 tablespoons Cocoa
Pouring Cream to mix
 (approx ¼ cup)

For the cake: melt butter and golden syrup together. Add eggs, sugar and vanilla essence and mix well. Dissolve baking soda in milk. Sift flour and cocoa, and add to the egg mixture alternately with the baking soda and milk. The result should be very runny.
Cook at 350°F (180°C) for 1 hour.
For the icing: mix ingredients together. Spread on cake.
Serve with whipped cream.

For any cake, using cream instead of water to wet the icing mixture makes for a really creamy icing. Chocolate icing made with cream will be a slightly lighter colour than if water is used.

HEATHER'S CRUNCHY TOPPED APPLE CAKE

CAKE
2 cups Self-Raising Flour
½ cup Wholemeal Self-Raising Flour
1 teaspoon Cinnamon
½ teaspoon Nutmeg
1 cup Sugar
185g Butter, melted
½ cup Water
3 Eggs, lightly beaten
3 Apples, peeled and sliced

TOPPING
60g Butter
½ cup Brown Sugar
¼ teaspoon Cinnamon
¼ teaspoon Nutmeg

For the cake: place wholemeal flour in bowl, add sifted flour, sugar
and spices. Mix in butter, water and eggs, and lastly add apples.
Pour into tin.
For the topping: melt butter and mix in dry ingredients.
Pour over cake mixture and cook for 1¼ hours at 350°F (180°C).

Serve warm with whipped cream.

CISS'S SPONGE CAKE

4 Eggs, separated
6 oz (170g) Caster Sugar
1 tablespoon Water
6 oz (170g) Cornflour
1 dessertspoon Flour
2 teaspoons Baking Powder
Pinch Salt
1 teaspoon Vanilla Essence

Using an electric beater, beat egg whites stiffly. Heat sugar and water in pot until boiling, stirring continuously. Add to egg whites and beat, then add yolks and vanilla.
Reduce beater speed and add sifted cornflour, flour, baking powder and salt a little at a time.
Bake in moderate oven about 20 minutes at 320°F (160°C).

Yes, those are the right quantities of ingredients!

"This is my mother's recipe. For my wedding to Fred in 1938, my mother made a four-tier wedding cake and my Aunty Muriel made 25 of these sponges – all beaten by hand and cooked in our family's range oven. They were all needed – the whole of Weymouth came!" - Dulcie

GINGER ALE FRUIT CAKE

½ pint (240ml) Ginger Ale
½ lb (225g) Sultanas
½ lb (225g) Dates
½ lb (225g) Currants
½ lb (225g) Raisins
2 tablespoons Lemon Rind
½ lb (225g) Butter
½ lb (225g) Sugar
4 Eggs
10 oz (280g) Flour
1 teaspoon Baking Powder
½ teaspoon Almond Essence
1 teaspoon Vanilla Essence
1 tablespoon Brandy

Soak fruit overnight in ginger ale.
Cream butter and sugar very well. Beat in eggs one at a time then
add sifted flour and baking powder.
Add soaked fruit and, lastly, essences and brandy.
Bake for 1½ to 2 hours in a paper-lined tin at 325°F (160°C).

"I used to send a fruit cake variation to my brothers serving overseas during World War II. It had no eggs in it but was laden with brandy, so it would keep." – Dulcie

ORANGE MADEIRA CAKE

CAKE
12 oz (340g) Sugar
12 oz (340g) Butter
Rind of 1 Orange
8 Eggs, beaten
½ cup Milk
Pinch Salt
2 large cups Flour
2 teaspoons Baking Powder

ICING
1½ cups Icing Sugar
2 tablespoons Butter
Juice and rind of 1 Orange
Boiling Water

For the cake: beat butter and sugar to a cream. Add orange rind, beaten eggs and then milk.
Sift all dry ingredients in separate bowl and fold through wet ingredients.
Bake in moderate oven at 350°F (180°C) for 1¼ hours.
For the icing: beat together icing sugar, butter and orange juice.
Add boiling water as required to reach a smooth consistency. Spread evenly over cooled cake.

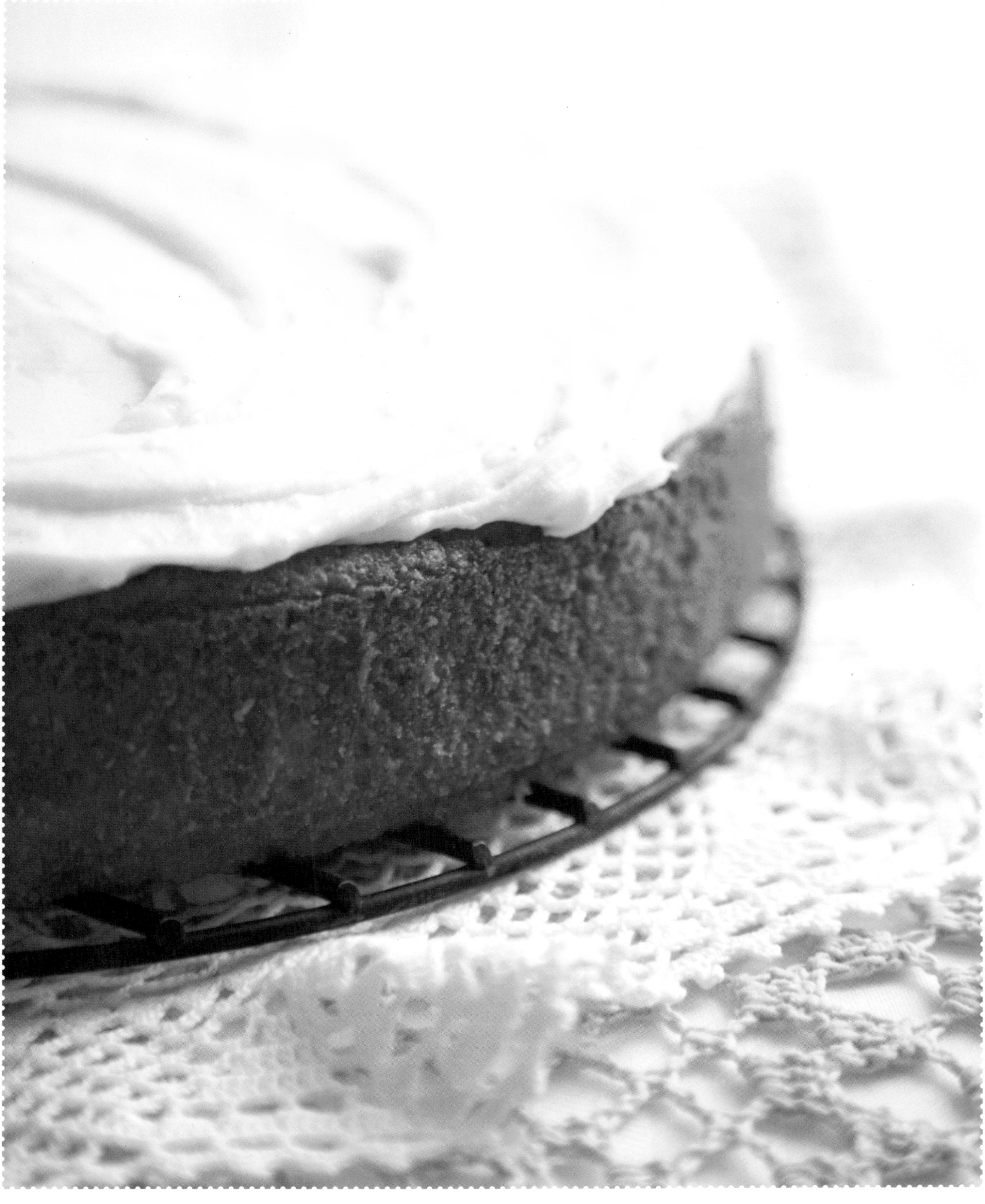

COFFEE CAKE

CAKE
2 tablespoons Strong Coffee Granules
3 oz (85g) Butter
5½ oz (155g) Sugar
1 teaspoon Vanilla Essence
3 Eggs, separated
5 oz (140g) Flour
1½ oz (42g) Cornflour
1 teaspoon Ginger
3 tablespoons Milk
1 teaspoon Baking Powder

ICING
2 cups Icing Sugar
2 tablespoons Butter
2 tablespoons Strong Coffee Granules
Boiling Water
½ cup Slivered Almonds

Whipped Cream to fill

For the cake: dissolve coffee in a little water. Cream butter, sugar, dissolved coffee and vanilla. Beat in egg yolks one at a time, then add sifted flour, cornflour and ginger, mixing in alternately with stiffly beaten egg whites. Mix well. Add milk and then baking powder. Bake for 20-30 minutes at 400°F (200°C).
For the icing: mix together icing sugar, butter and coffee, adding boiling water to make a smooth consistency.
When the cake is cool, cut in half and fill with whipped cream, then ice and sprinkle slivered almonds on top.

Bottled Spagetti & Tomato

10 lb Tomatoes   3/4 oz Salt
5 ozs Sugar   1/2-1 teaspoon pepper
16 ozs Onions   14 oz Spagetti

Skin tomatoes. Slice into pan with
finely chopped onions. Add sugar, salt,
pepper. Simmer 15-20 mins. Cook
spagetti in boiling salted water. Drain &
add to tomatoes. Boil together for 10 mins.
Place in sterilized jars. leaving 1 in
head space. Seal & process in a
Water Bath for 1½ hours at boiling
point.

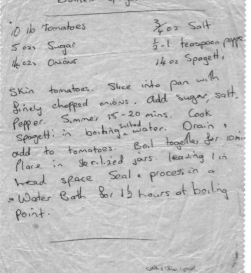

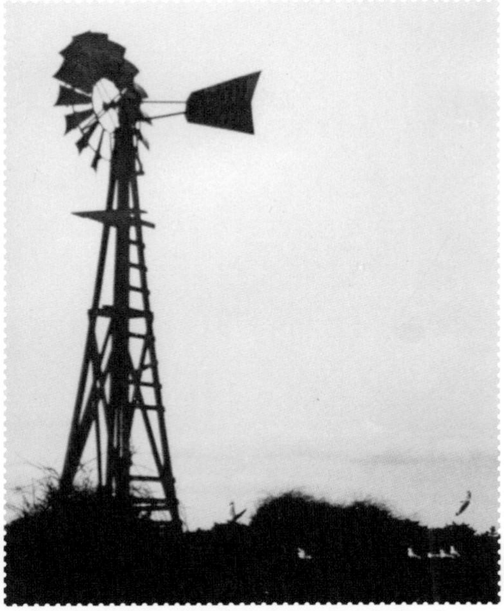
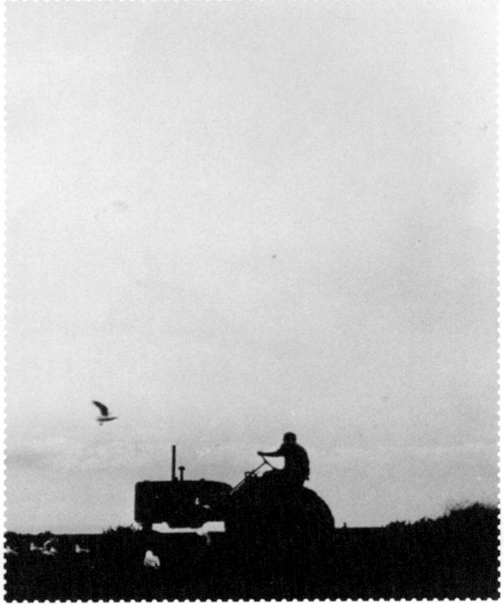
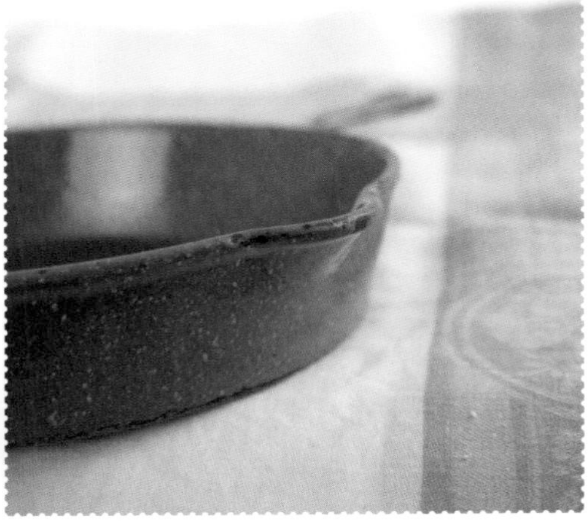
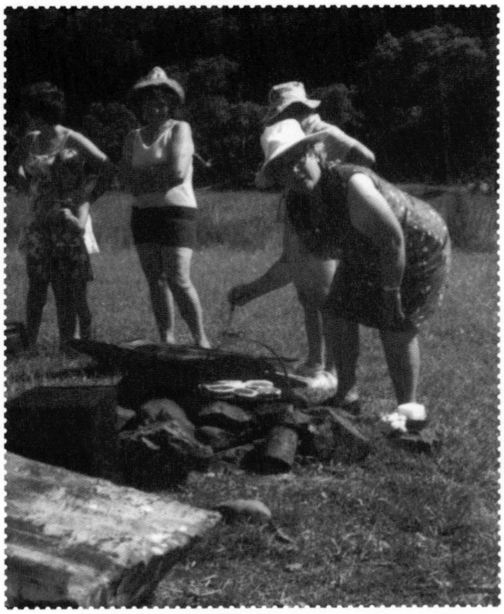
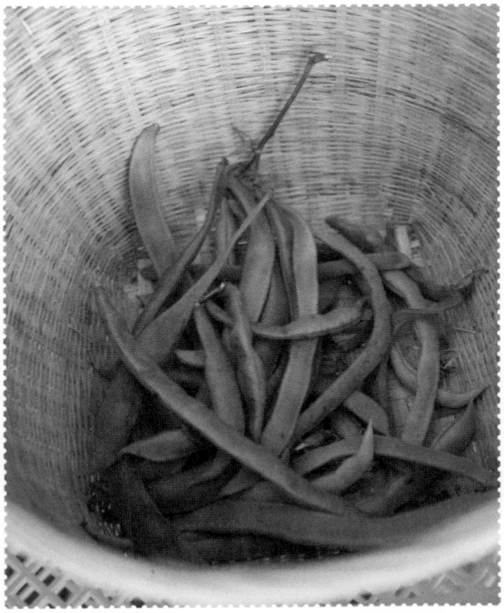
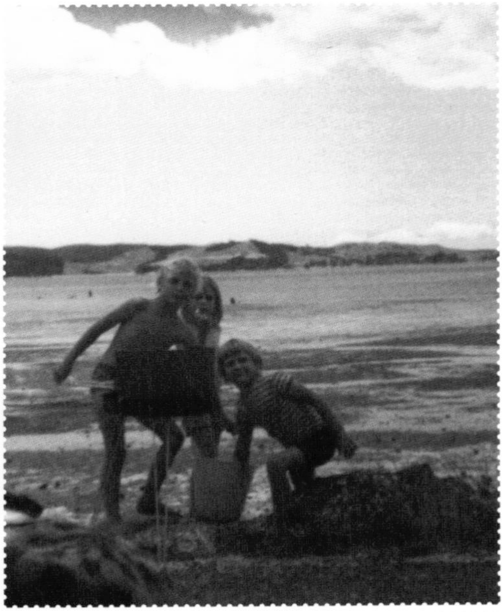

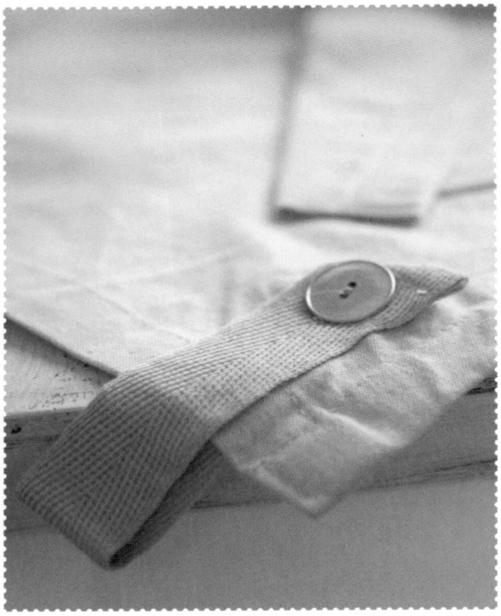

"Fred was working as a leading stockman down south after the war, but soon he said he wanted to give it up to go fishing. I nearly died, because sometimes the fish don't bite; sometimes the weather's rough and you can't go out.

But I said 'if you help me, I'll help you. On rainy days, you can look after the house and I'll sew.' And that's what we did. I was a self-taught dressmaker and I mostly made bridal gowns for people. And Fred liked looking after the house while I did that.

On those rainy days, he might put the vegies in a pot for me, but I still did most of the cooking. Fred was easy to please — he ate everything — but he didn't want 'airy fairy' food. It had to be good and hearty."

- Dulcie

FRED'S DINNERS

WINTER SLICE

3 Bacon Rashers
1 large Potato
1 large Onion
1 cup Cauliflower
3 Eggs
1 cup Flour
2 teaspoons Baking Powder
½ cup Oil
1 cup Milk
1 cup Tasty Cheese, grated
Salt and Pepper

Dice bacon and fry. Peel, chop and steam vegetables.
In a separate bowl, beat eggs and lightly stir in flour, baking powder
and oil until smooth. Add milk, vegetables, bacon, cheese and
seasoning, and mix to combine.
Pour into greased baking dish and place in oven for 30 minutes at
375°F (190°C).

CREAM OF FISH SOUP

2 Fresh Fish Heads (preferably Snapper)
1 Onion, roughly chopped
Milk
Flour to thicken
Salt and Pepper
1 good teaspoon Worcestershire Sauce
Parsley to serve

Place fish heads in saucepan with onion, and cover with water. Boil
1 hour, then strain. Take strained liquid and add an equal quantity
of milk. Return to heat and thicken with a little flour.
Add salt, pepper and worcestershire sauce.
Add a small handful of finely chopped fresh parsley to serve.

*A knob of butter added right at the end makes all the difference to
the taste.*

**"When my children had tests at school, they
would ask for fish soup the day before, as fish
is good for the brain. I use only parsley and
onion as too many vegetables spoil the delicate
flavour of fresh fish." - Dulcie**

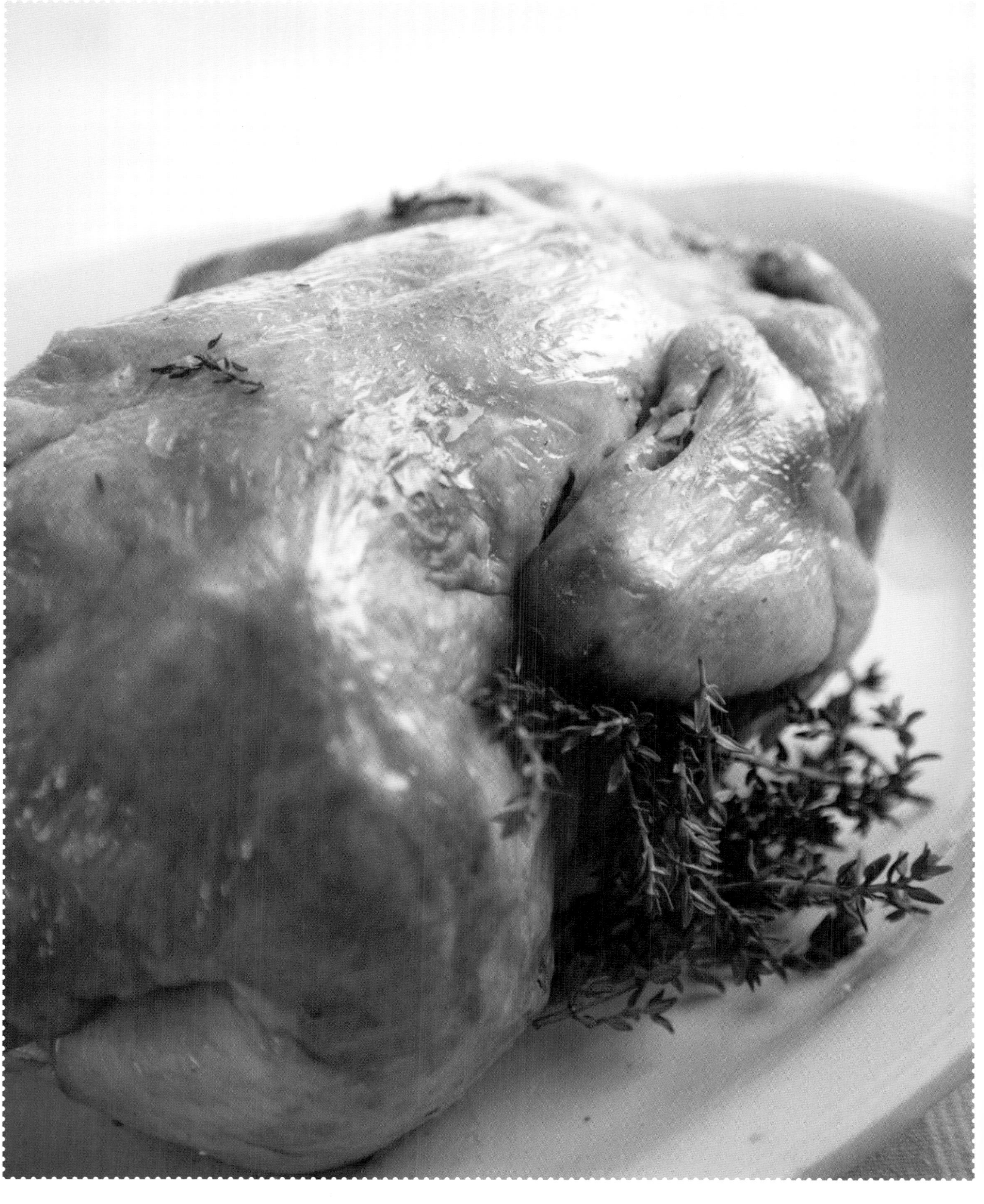

ROAST CHICKEN
WITH THYME AND ONION STUFFING

4 Small Onions
Small bunch Thyme
Salt
3 cups Fresh Breadcrumbs
1 Apple, peeled and sliced
2 tablespoons Dripping or Butter
Pepper
1 Organic Chicken

Peel and slice onions and put in a pan with the thyme. Cover with cold water, add seasoning of salt, and boil until onions are tender, then drain well.
Mix apple, breadcrumbs and butter lightly together, and then add onions to this mixture. Season with pepper.
Wash and dry chicken inside and out. Stuff chicken with thyme and onion mix, and secure with skewer. Place in roasting pan.
Cook at 400°F (200°C) for 10 minutes then reduce heat to 350°F (180°C) for 1 hour and 50 minutes, or until juices run clear.

"When I was growing up, chicken was only for special occasions – Christmas, weddings and birthdays. Wringing their necks was a man's job, and then the women would pluck and gut them." - Dulcie

FISH PIE SUPREME

2 lb (900g) Potatoes
2 oz (55g) Butter
½ pint (240ml) Milk
Salt and Pepper
1 tablespoon Flour
2 teaspoons Parsley, chopped
2 Eggs, hard boiled and chopped
1 lb (455g) Smoked Fish, flaked

Peel, cook and mash potatoes, mixing in half the butter and a little milk. Season with salt and pepper. Melt remaining butter in a saucepan, add flour, and gradually add milk. Stir until mixture thickens and cook for 4–5 minutes. Add parsley, chopped eggs and fish. Line a pie dish with mashed potatoes, fill with fish mixture and pile remainder of potatoes on top. Heat through and brown potatoes on top.
Serve very hot.

CORNISH PASTIES

2 medium Potatoes
1 large Onion
½ lb (225g) Raw Steak
½ cup Beef Stock
Salt, Pepper and Cayenne Pepper
¼ cup Peas
400g packet Short Pastry
Milk for brushing

Dice peeled potatoes, onion and meat. Place all in a pot with beef stock and season to taste with salt and peppers. Bring to the boil and simmer for 45 minutes on a low heat. Remove from heat and add peas to hot mixture. Leave to cool.
Roll out pastry. Cut into fairly large rounds using a saucer to gauge size. Place a small portion of meat and vegetable on top of each round. Wet the edges of the pastry and join them on the top of the meat. Crimp the edges. Place pasties on a cold scone tray. Brush with milk. Bake at 375°F (190°C) for 30–40 minutes.

Makes 4.

NANA RITA'S COTTAGE PIE

SAVOURY PASTRY
1 cup Flour
Pinch Salt
50g Butter
¼ cup Tasty Cheese, grated
½ cup Ice Cold Water

TOPPING
4 large Potatoes, mashed
Tasty Cheese, grated
1 Tomato, sliced

FILLING
Oil for frying
350g Beef Mince
1 large tablespoon Curry Powder
Garlic to taste
2 tablespoons Tomato Sauce
1 large Carrot
1 large Onion
½ cup Parsley, chopped
½ cup Frozen Peas
Salt and Pepper

For the pastry: sift flour and salt together. Rub in butter, add grated cheese and mix with the water. Roll out dough and line your greased pie dish with pastry. Stand in fridge for 15-20 minutes.
Bake blind — line pastry with baking paper and fill with dried beans or rice and cook for 15 minutes at 430°F (220°C).
For the filling: heat oil in saucepan, add mince, garlic, curry powder and tomato sauce. Just heat through, then add vegetables, finely chopped. Cover with water and cook about 20 minutes on medium heat, then thicken with flour. Lastly add parsley and peas and leave to cool.
Add cold filling to cooked pie shell. Top with mashed potatoes, cheese and tomato slices. Place under hot grill until golden brown.

Very tasty served with a fresh salad.

DEEP-FRIED SCALLOPS

1 Dozen Fresh Scallops
Oil for deep frying

BATTER
4 oz (115g) Flour
Pinch Salt
1 Egg
½ cup Tepid Milk
1 tablespoon Salad Oil

Sift salt and flour, break in egg, add milk gradually, beating all the time. Add salad oil. Beat the batter until smooth. Stand for 1 hour if possible, then use as desired.
Wash and dry scallops. Coat in flour, then in batter.
Heat oil in frying pan. When it's hot, place scallops in pan and deep fry until golden brown.

"At one time, Fred and I owned a fish and chip shop, where the whole family helped out to sell Fred's daily catch. This is the batter we used in the shop." - Dulcie

BOTTLED SPAGHETTI

10 lb (4.5kg) Tomatoes
14 oz (400g) Onions
5 oz (140g) Sugar
2 teaspoons Salt
½ teaspoon Pepper
14 oz (400g) Dry Spaghetti

Skin tomatoes (see method on page 26). Slice into pan with finely
chopped onions. Add sugar, salt and pepper. Simmer 15-20 minutes.
Cook spaghetti in boiling salted water. Drain and add to tomatoes.
Boil together for 10 minutes and place in sterilised jars, leaving a
1 inch (2.5cm) space.

"When stores first started selling tinned
spaghetti, Gran thought, 'I could do that'.
So she did. It's simple, but very effective — as
kids, we were never allowed as much as we
wanted, because the adults ate more than their
fair share!" - Natalie

PIPI FRITTERS

½ cup Flour
1 teaspoon Baking Powder
Salt and Pepper
2 Eggs, separated
¼ cup Chilled Water
1 cup Pipis, chopped
Oil for frying

Mix flour, baking powder, salt and pepper in a bowl. In a separate bowl, whisk the egg yolks and water together, then gently add this to the dry ingredients. Fold pipis into mixture. Whisk egg whites and fold them in also.
Heat oil in pan and place spoonfuls of mixture to desired size in oil. Cook for 1 to 2 minutes each side or until cooked through. This depends on how thin you have made your fritters.

"We would gather pipis from the Manukau Harbour and barbeque them there and then on the beach. Sometimes there wouldn't be any left to make fritters when we got home!" - Dulcie

STEAK & ONION PIE

FILLING
500g Blade Steak
4 large Potatoes
1 large Onion
Salt and Pepper
1 cup Beef Stock

PASTRY
½ lb (225g) Flour
1 tablespoon Baking Powder
Pinch Salt
3oz (85g) Butter
Water

For the filling: Slice potatoes and onion, and finely slice the steak. Line bottom of pie dish with sliced potatoes and cover with the steak, salt, pepper and onion. Put another layer of potatoes on top. Pour beef stock over everything. Cook for 1 hour and 15 minutes at 320°F (160°C).

For the pastry: sift dry ingredients in a bowl. Rub in butter then add water to make stiff dough. Roll out ¼ inch thick and cover filling. Bake at 400°F (200°C) for a further 20 minutes.

PIZZA

BASE
2 cups Flour
1 cup Wholemeal Flour
2 teaspoons Baking Powder
1 teaspoon Salt
4 - 6 tablespoons Butter
½ - 1 cup Milk

TOPPING
1 large tin (820g) Spaghetti
2 medium Onions
8 Bacon Rashers, chopped
1 tin (439g) Pineapple or ½ Fresh Pineapple, chopped
2 cups Cheese, grated

For the base: mix flours, baking powder and salt. Rub in butter.
Roll out into large square on baking tray.
For the topping: place all ingredients on top of pizza base in the
order they appear above.
Place tray in oven at 410°F (210°C) for 20 minutes.

CHICKEN CASSEROLE

12 Chicken Wings
6 Pickling Onions, cut in half
1 large Potato, peeled and diced
2 Carrots, peeled and diced
Small bunch Thyme
½ cup Water
Salt and Pepper to taste

Wash chicken wings in cold salted water and pat dry. Place all ingredients into a large pot with lid on and gently simmer until cooked, for about 35 minutes.

No evening meal was complete without dessert, even if it were simply home-bottled peaches and cream. On occasion, that was all Dulcie had time for – she was kept busy as the neighbourhood hairdresser and cake decorator as well as dressmaker, not to mention maker of wedding shoes and hats for flower girls.

Her brides would bring her a picture of the dress they wanted, and Dulcie would think out the patterns in bed before she went to sleep. Then they would take the train into Queen Street together and go shopping for the required silk, voile, lace, satin or georgette. Dulcie sewed the dress on her mother's treadle machine and at the final fitting, Fred was always the chief judge. "I put my heart and soul into every one I made," says Dulcie. Her fee was three pounds and a photo of the bride in her dress on her wedding day.

DESERTS

APRICOT SPONGE

2 oz (55g) Butter
2 oz (55g) Brown Sugar
1 Egg
2 oz (55g) Flour
1 teaspoon Baking Powder
1 bottle or 2 tins (850g) Stewed Apricots

Cream butter and sugar, add egg and beat well. Add sifted flour and baking powder. Place hot stewed apricots into dish and pour sponge mixture over them.
Bake for 40 minutes at 400°F (200°C).

Other fruits can be used in place of the apricots if desired.

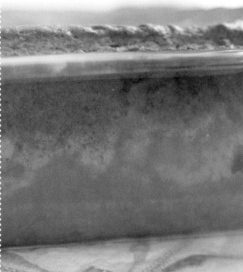

BAKED CUSTARD

PER PERSON:
1 Egg
1 cup Milk
1 dessertspoon Sugar
Nutmeg, grated
A little Butter

Beat the egg slightly, add milk and sugar, pour into pie dish. Add grating of nutmeg and a few tiny pieces of butter. Place pie dish in a pan of cold water. If time allows, the custard is improved by standing in the cold water for several hours before being baked.
Put pan containing dish and water in the oven at 350°F (180°C) until custard is firm and brown, about 30–40 minutes. Do not let water boil.

Other spices such as cinnamon can also be added with the nutmeg.

PUMPKIN PIE

PASTRY
1 lb (455g) Butter
¾ teaspoon Salt
4 cups Flour
4 teaspoon Baking Powder
1 tablespoon Castor Sugar
¾ cup Water
1 tablespoon Vinegar
1 Egg White for brushing

FILLING
1 cup Pumpkin, cooked, mashed and sieved
2 Egg Yolks
½ cup Brown Sugar
¼ teaspoon Salt
½ teaspoon Ginger
½ teaspoon Nutmeg
Pinch All Spice
½ teaspoon Cinnamon
1½ cups Milk
1 Egg White

For the pastry: rub butter into flour, salt, sugar and baking powder to resemble bread crumbs. Add water and vinegar to form a soft dough. Roll out on floured board to desired size and place in greased pie dish. Leave in fridge for 30 minutes.
For the filling: mix pumpkin, sugar, spices, salt and egg yolks, then add milk. Fold in stiffly-beaten egg white.
Brush pastry in dish with egg white, then pour filling mixture on top. Bake in hot oven (400°F, 200°C) for about 15 minutes, then moderate oven (350°F, 180°C) until baked (approximately another 25 minutes).

DULCIE'S FAMOUS CHRISTMAS PUDDING

PUDDING
5 large cups Flour
2 lbs (900g) Sultanas
1 lb (455g) Currants
1 lb (455g) Raisins
1½ ozs (42g) Lemon Peel, finely chopped
1 lb (455g) Suet (Shortening)
1 teaspoon Salt
4 teaspoons Baking Powder
4 Eggs
1 lb (455g) Raw Sugar
2 teaspoons Vanilla
1 tablespoon Golden Syrup
2 cups Milk
2 cups Water

NUTMEG SAUCE
3 tablespoons Butter
6 flat tablespoons Flour
4 tablespoons Sugar
½ teaspoon Salt
1½ Whole Nutmegs, grated
¼ cup Cold Water
2 cups Boiling Water

"Gran always made sure only the best quality dried fruit went into this mix, and she would put the pudding on to boil before she went to church early on Christmas morning. Several hours later, when it was finally served up, it was the supreme highlight of the year for us all, surpassing all the other goodies from Gran's kitchen!" - Natalie

For the pudding: mix flour, fruit, suet, salt and baking powder. In another bowl, beat eggs and raw sugar, then add golden syrup and vanilla to eggs. Mix egg mixture into dry ingredients, adding milk and water at same time, mix well. Scald cloth and flour it. Put mixture into it and tie with room to swell. Boil - fully immersed in water - for 6-7 hours adding boiling water as it steams away.
For the sauce: mix butter, flour, sugar, salt and grated nutmeg together. Gradually add enough cold water to mix to a smooth paste.
Add boiling water, stirring all the time at a low heat, until you reach a clear consistency.
Simmer for 5 minutes.

SPANISH CREAM

½ oz (14g) Gelatine
1 pint (570ml) Milk
3 Eggs, separated
3 tablespoons Sugar
Vanilla Essence

Soak gelatine in milk for 1 hour. Put in pan and let it come to boil, stirring all the time. Beat yolks with sugar, add to milk, stir until it thickens. Take off heat and cool. Add stiffly-beaten whites and essence. Pour into mould, and place into fridge to set.

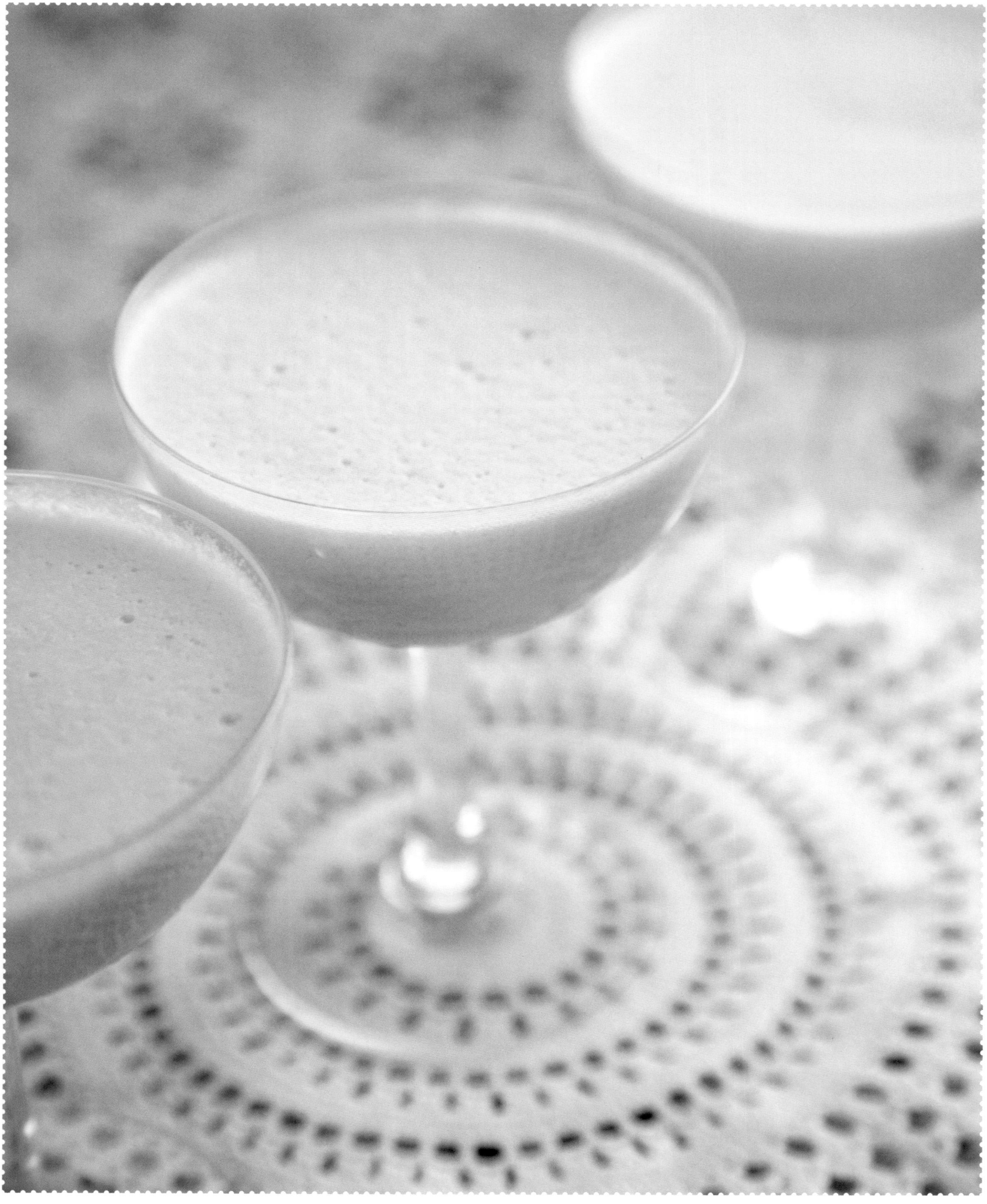

APPLE PIE

FILLING
8 Apples, peeled and sliced
½ cup Sugar
2 tablespoons Water

PASTRY
¾ lb (340g) Butter
½ teaspoon Salt
3 cups Flour
3 teaspoons Baking Powder
½ cup Cold Water
1 tablespoon Vinegar

For the filling: place apple, sugar and water into a pot and cook for 15 minutes. Leave to cool.
For the pastry: rub butter into flour, baking powder and salt. Add water and vinegar to make a soft dough. Divide in half, for lining and lid. Roll out each half on a floured surface to desired size.
Line your pie tin with pastry then add apple filling.
Wet edges of pastry and place the second pastry disc on top. Crimp the edges to hold pastry together.
Brush top with milk and bake for 30 minutes at 400°F (200°C).

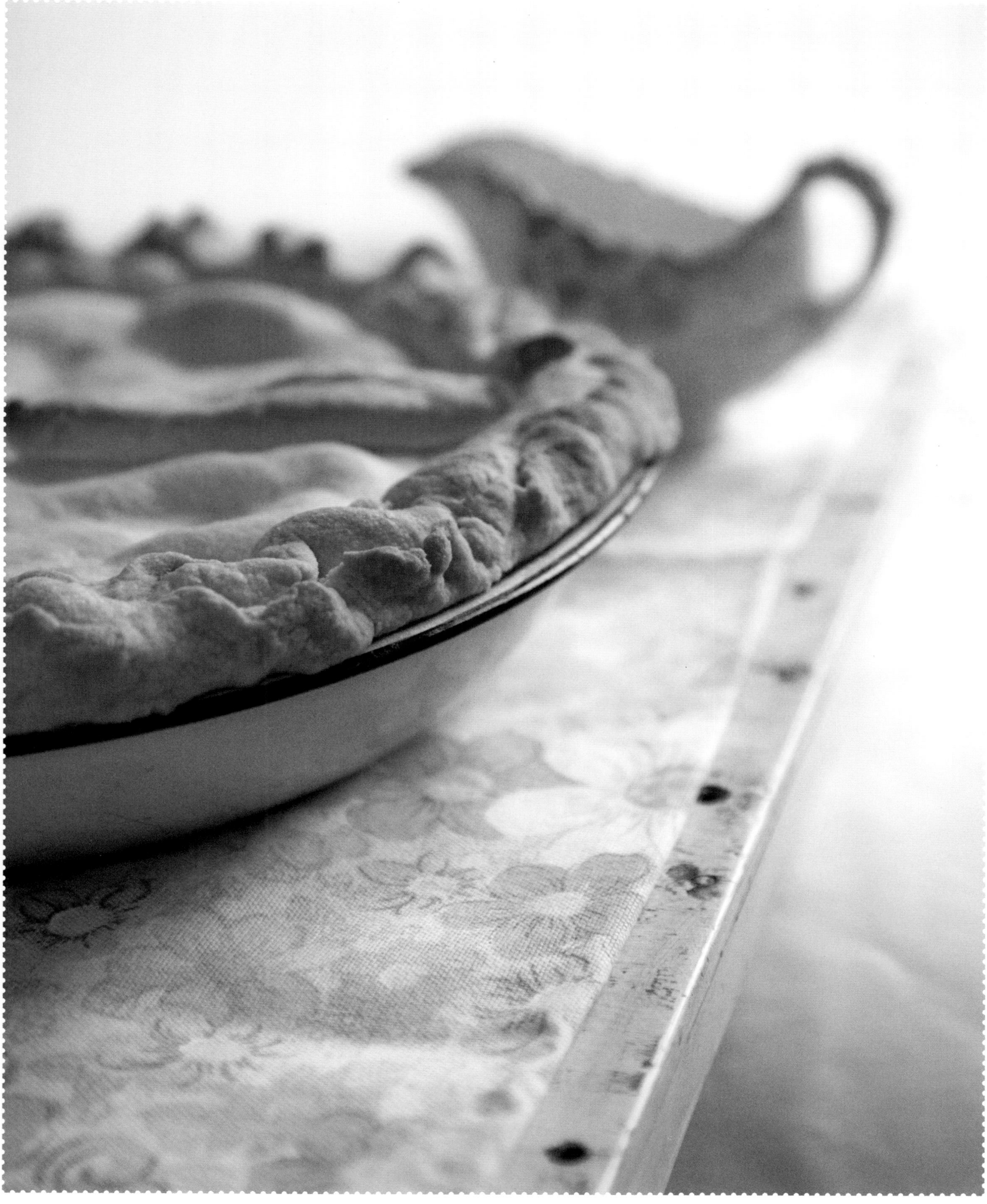

CARAMEL HAZELNUT PUDDING

1 cup Flour
1 teaspoon Baking Powder
¼ cup Hazelnuts, finely chopped
1 tin (400ml) Sweetened Condensed Milk
1 tablespoon Butter
1 teaspoon Vanilla Essence
½ cup Milk
1 cup Brown Sugar
1¾ cup Boiling Water

Sift the flour and baking powder into a bowl and stir in finely chopped hazelnuts. Set aside.
Place the condensed milk in a pan and stir over medium heat for approximately 10 minutes or until golden brown.
Stir the butter, vanilla essence and milk into the condensed milk. Leave mixture to cool slightly. Pour into the dry ingredients and mix well.
Pour mixture into greased dish. Sprinkle the brown sugar on top of mixture and then carefully pour the boiling water over it all.
Bake at 350°F (180°C) for 45 minutes.

LEMON MERINGUE PIE

PASTRY
1½ cups Plain Flour
1 tablespoon Icing Sugar
150g Cold Butter, chopped
1 Egg Yolk
2 tablespoons Cold Water

MERINGUE
4 Egg Whites
½ cup Castor Sugar
½ teaspoon Vinegar

LEMON FILLING
1 cup Castor Sugar
1 cup Cold Water
¼ cup Lemon Juice
1 tablespoon Butter
Pinch Salt
3½ tablespoons Cornflour
2 Egg Yolks (3 is plentiful)
Rind of 1 Lemon, finely grated

For the pastry: combine flour, icing sugar and butter, and knead by hand. Add egg yolk and cold water to form a dough. Roll out to desired size and place in greased tin. Leave in fridge for 30 minutes. Line pastry with baking paper and fill with dried beans or rice and cook for 15 minutes at 430°F (220°C). Remove paper and beans/rice from pie shell and bake a further 10 minutes. Cool.

For the filling: put sugar, 1 cup of water, butter, lemon juice and salt into a pan and bring just to boiling point. Mix cornflour with enough extra water to make a sloppy paste and add to syrup. Stir continuously until mixture thickens on medium heat, and then leave to simmer without stirring for another 5 minutes on very low heat. Take from heat, let cool slightly, then add beaten egg yolks and return to low heat for a few minutes. Stir briskly. Add grated lemon rind. Pour mixture into baked pastry shell.

For the meringue: whip the whites till very stiff and fluffy. Add the sugar very gradually, beating vigorously. Add vinegar and mix well. Pour over lemon filling in pastry shell.

Bake at 350°F (180°C) for 10-15 minutes or until tinged with brown.

RHUBARB CRUMBLE

5 cups Rhubarb, chopped

CRUMBLE
1 cup Rolled Oats
Pinch Salt
¾ cup Flour
1 cup Brown Sugar
½ cup Melted Butter

SAUCE
1 cup Sugar
1 cup Water
2 tablespoons Cornflour
½ teaspoon Vanilla

Mix crumble ingredients and divide in half. Line dish with half the mixture and place cut rhubarb on top.
Mix sauce ingredients in a pan and heat over slow heat until sugar is dissolved.
Pour sauce over rhubarb, then cover the whole with the other half of the crumble mixture.
Bake at 375°F (190° C) for 30-40 minutes.

RASPBERRY FLUFF

1 packet Raspberry Jelly Crystals
1 cup Boiling Water
2 Egg Whites
2 tablespoons Sugar
¼ teaspoon Cream of Tartar

Soak jelly crystals in 1 cup of boiling water. Stir and leave to cool.
Whip the egg whites with sugar and cream of tartar. Add to jelly
and whip until fluffy.
Set in mould.

TRIFLE

SPONGE
3 Eggs
Pinch Salt
6 oz (170g) Sugar
4 oz (115g) Flour
1 teaspoon Baking Powder
2 oz (55g) Melted Butter
2 tablespoons Boiling Water

FILLINGS
Raspberry Jam
Whipped Cream
1 tin (375g) Bottled Peaches
Sherry or Fruit Juice from Stewed Fruit
Flaked Almonds for decoration

CUSTARD
3 tablespoons Custard Powder
1 Egg
3 tablespoons Sugar
600ml Milk

"If we were eating custard on its own, I would stir it for a few minutes with a sprig of fresh peach leaves from the orchard to add flavour, and then pour it into bowls, adding a teaspoon or two of freshly made jam in the centre of each." - Dulcie

For the sponge: beat eggs with salt then slowly add sugar and beat until thick. Gently fold in sifted flour and baking powder. Lastly add melted butter and boiling water. Bake in greased square tin for 25-30 minutes at 375°F (190°C).

For the custard: place custard powder, egg and sugar into bowl. Mix in enough milk to make a smooth paste. Heat remaining milk until nearly boiling. Add custard paste to milk, stirring constantly until thick. Do not boil. Set aside to cool.

Cut cold sponge cake into squares and spread with raspberry jam. Place cake into glass dish. Place peaches on top of sponge, add enough sherry or fruit juice to soften sponge and then pour over the cooled custard. Cover with whipped cream. Decorate with almonds.

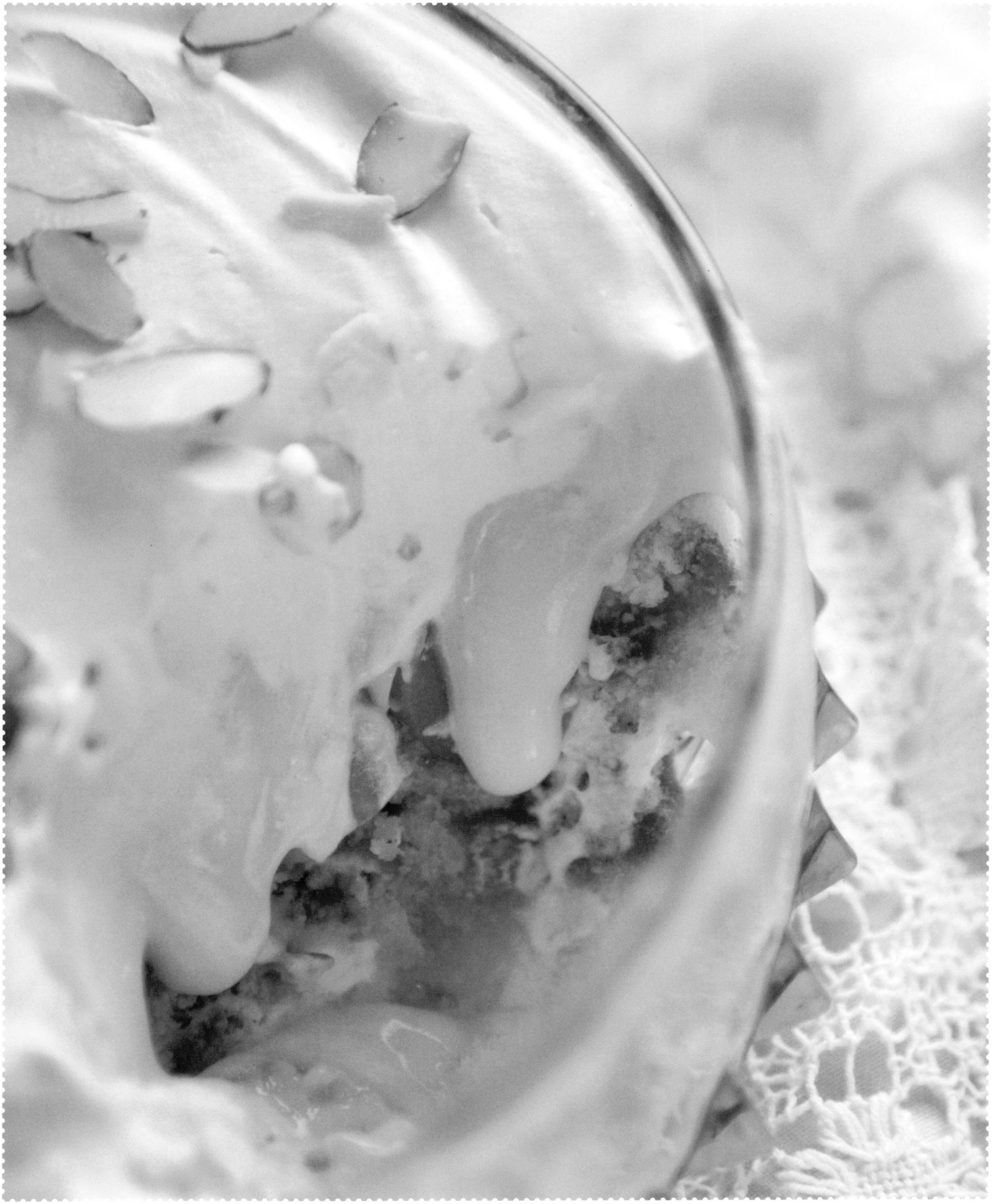

Value of Blackberries.

Blackberries are very beneficial in case of dysentry. The berries are healthful eating. Tea made of the roots & leaves are good. The syrup made from the berries is excellent.

Apricot Jam.

To 3lbs dried apricots add 10 pts. water. Soak 48 hrs. & add 11 lbs. sugar & boil about 2 hrs. Or soak 24 hrs. & boil 1½ hrs. without sugar then add sugar & boil 1¼ hrs.

"When our house was built in the 1940s, I had shelves made especially for the preserves - the builders nicknamed me the 'cupboard lady'. Fred and I had a market garden, and also an orchard where we grew staples like apples and citrus, but also passionfruit, blackberry vines, guavas and cape gooseberries.

Harvest time was hectic, as the fruit had to be picked and preserved at just the right time, just this side of ripe. Plums would be ready on their own, but the peaches and pears ripened at the same time as each other. Fred would help me pick the fruit, and if there wasn't as much as we wanted, we would buy an extra 40 pound case of it.

Then, because we were so busy with all our usual work during the day, I would stay up all night bottling fruit. I would do this two or three times a season. Sometimes I would get as little as 40 minutes sleep before getting up to see to the children's breakfast the next day." - Dulcie

PRESERVES AND SAUCES

RASPBERRY JAM

7 lbs (3.2kg) Fresh Raspberries
7 lbs (3.2kg) Sugar

Heat berries (without water) over medium heat until they boil.
Stir in the sugar gradually. Boil for around 5 minutes.
Pour into sterilised jars and seal while still hot.

*Frozen berries can be used, but produce extra liquid which needs
to be drained after boiling.*

TOMATO SAUCE

9 lb (4kg) Tomatoes
4 lb (1.8kg) Apples
2 lb (900g) Onions
½ oz (14g) Peppercorns
½ oz (14g) Chillies
½ oz (14g) Cloves
3 lb (1.4kg) Brown Sugar
½ lb (225g) Salt
3 pints (1.7 litres) Vinegar

Roughly chop (but don't peel) tomatoes, apples and onions.
Tie peppercorns, chillies and cloves in muslin.
Boil all ingredients steadily for 3 hours, then discard muslin
ingredients and strain the rest through a colander.
Bottle. Can be used immediately.

PASSIONFRUIT BUTTER

16 Passionfruit
2 large tablespoons Butter
4 Eggs, lightly beaten
2 cups Sugar

Remove fruit pulp from skins and put it into a saucepan with sugar, eggs and butter. Stir mixture over fire until thick but do not let it boil. When cold, put into sterilised jars and cover.

"If you don't have a fire handy as Gran did in the 1930s, low heat on a stove top works fine as a substitute!" – Natalie

APRICOT JAM

1½ lbs (685g) Dried Apricots
5 pints (10 cups) Water
5½ lbs (2.5kg) Sugar

Soak apricots in water for 48 hours. Add sugar and boil for about
2 hours. Pour into sterilised jars and seal while still hot.

MUSTARD PICKLE

6 cups Vegetables, such as:
Onions
Cucumber
Butterbeans
Green Tomatoes
Carrots
Medium Cauliflower

½ cup Salt
6 cups Water
½ cup Sugar
½ cup Flour
2 tablespoons Mustard
1 tablespoon Tumeric
1 tablespoon Curry Powder
½ teaspoon Cayenne Pepper
2 quarts (2.25 litres) Vinegar

Dissolve salt in water and soak vegetables in resulting brine for
24 hours. Drain and set aside.
Mix flour, sugar, mustard, turmeric, curry powder and cayenne
pepper in a large pot. Stir in a small amount of vinegar to create a
smooth paste. Gradually add remaining vinegar. Bring to the boil,
stirring until thick. Add the vegetables and boil for 5 minutes.
Pour into sterilised jars and seal.

Once sealed, leave for at least three weeks before opening.

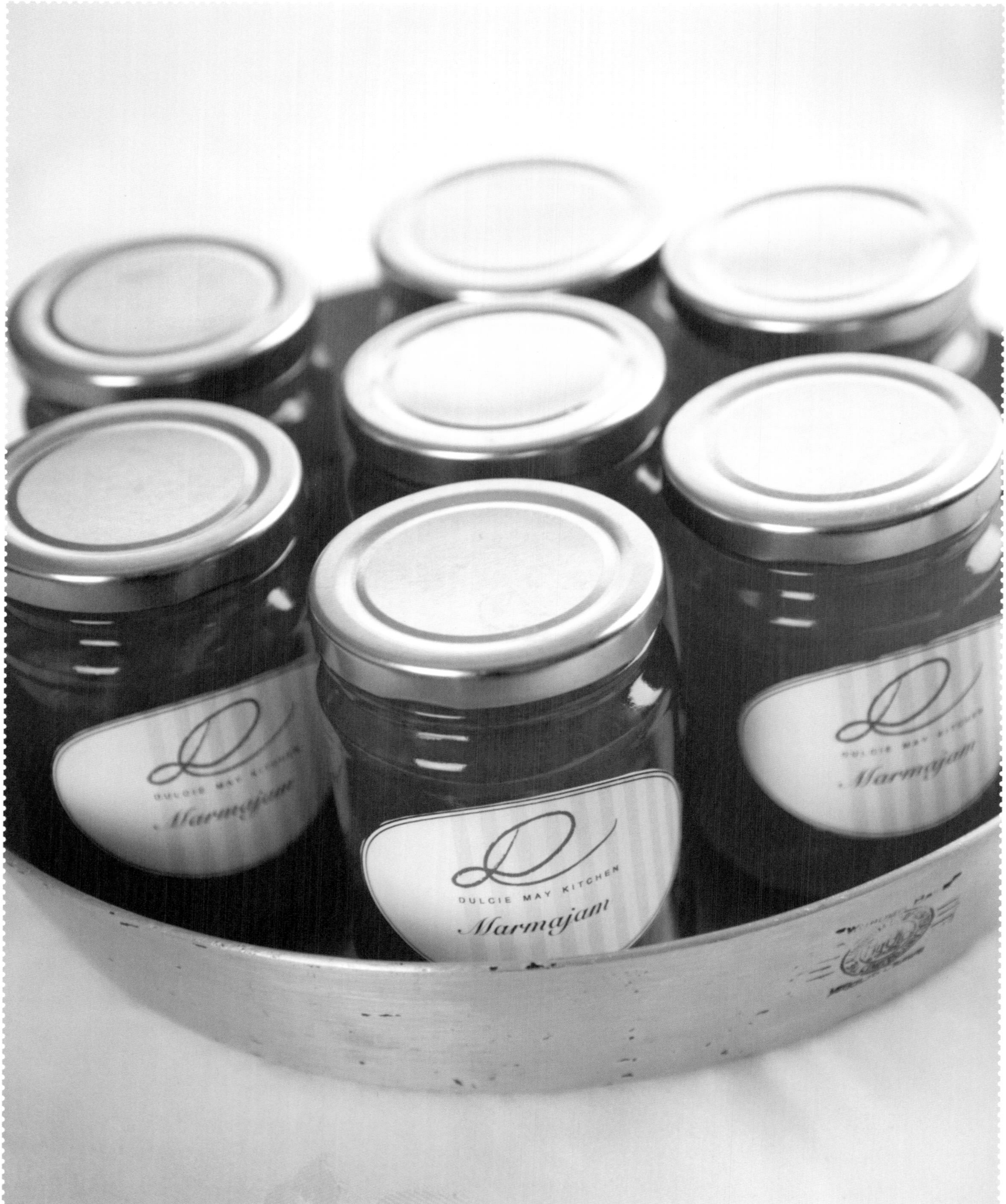
DULCIE MAY KITCHEN
Marmajam

MARMAJAM

4 lbs (1.8 kg) Fruit - Grapefruit and Orange
Rind of 1 Lemon
12 cups Water
8 lbs (3.6 kg) Sugar
Pinch Salt

Slice fruit *extremely* finely. Put in pot with rind and water and leave to soak overnight. Place on heat and bring to the boil then simmer until the fruit skin is very soft. Gradually add sugar and bring to the boil again. Boil only until the mixture sets when tested — this won't take long.
Add salt before pouring into sterilised jars.

Do not be afraid to mix different fruits.

"It's nice to create things. Like marmajam - I love to give it to those who love it." – Dulcie

BOTTLED FRUIT

Peaches or Pears

SYRUP
Thin syrup – 1 cup of sugar to 3 cups of water
Medium syrup – 1 cup of sugar to 2 cups of water
Thick syrup – 1 cup of sugar to 1 cup of water
Very rich syrup – 2 cups of sugar to 1 cup of water

Peel desired amount of fruit and steam for about 8 minutes. Leave
whole, or cut into halves or slices. Pack the fruit into hot jars or
bottles as tightly as possible without bruising the fruit.
For the syrup: boil sugar and water together until sugar has dissolved.
Stir occasionally.
Completely cover fruit with hot syrup, and to within half an inch
(1.5cm) of top of jar.
Screw lids on tightly and wipe bottles clean with damp cloth.

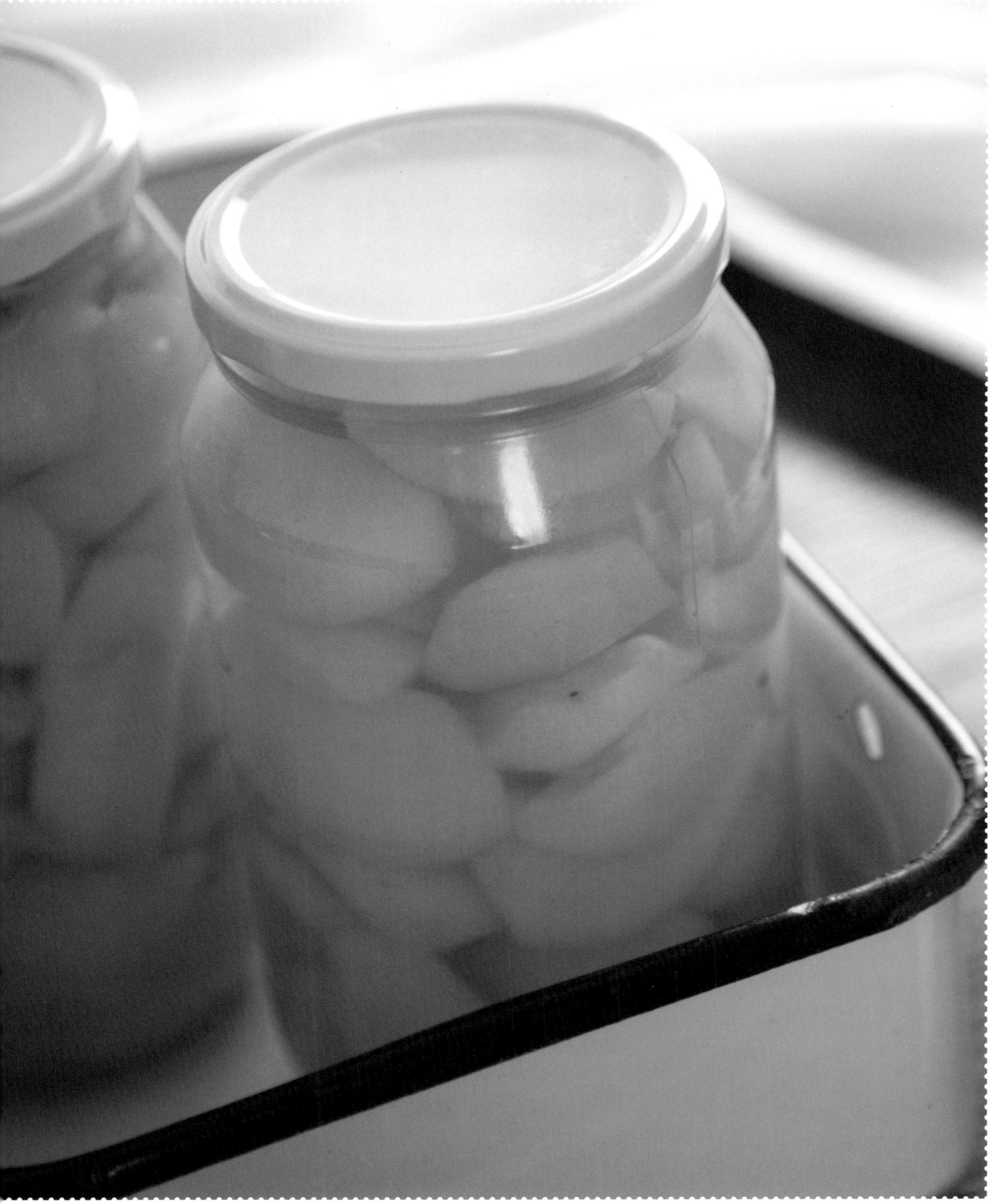

MINT JELLY

8 tablespoons Sugar
2 cups Vinegar
1 packet Lime Jelly Crystals
½ cup Sherry
30 large Mint Leaves, chopped

Heat vinegar, sugar and jelly crystals until sugar and crystals are dissolved. Add sherry and mint. Mix well. Seal in sterilised jars and place in fridge to set.
Give the jars a shake roughly every ½ hour, so that the mint is set floating in the jelly.

HONEY DRESSING

3 tablespoons Honey
2 tablespoons Lemon Juice
4 tablespoons Olive Oil
Salt and Pepper to taste

Mix all ingredients together and beat well.

Herbs can be added for variety.

WHITE SAUCE

1 tablespoon Butter
1 tablespoon Flour
1 cup Milk
Salt and Pepper to taste

Melt butter in a saucepan, stir in the flour, add the milk gradually, stirring all the time. Lastly add pepper and salt. Cook at least 5 minutes on low heat.

Parsley Sauce – Add 1 tablespoon chopped parsley.
Onion Sauce – Add 1 or 2 cooked chopped onions.
Cheese Sauce – Add 1 cup of tasty cheese.

GRAVY

Fat from Roast Meat
1 tablespoon Flour
1 pint Vegetable, Beef or Chicken Stock

When meat is cooked, remove from pan, and pour off nearly all the fat. Stir in flour, add stock, and bring to the boil, stirring constantly. Strain into gravy boat.

MAYONNAISE

2 Eggs
Pinch Salt
2 tablespoons Sugar
1 teaspoons Mustard
1 tablespoon Flour
Small Piece of Butter
1 cup Vinegar
1½ cups Water

Beat eggs, salt, sugar, mustard, flour and butter together. Add vinegar and water. Boil until thick and bottle. Just before serving, add a little milk if a thinner consistency is required.

CONVERSION CHARTS

WEIGHT EQUIVALENTS

1/4 oz.	7 grams
1/2 oz.	14 grams
1 oz.	28 grams
2 oz.	55 grams
4 oz.	115 grams
8 oz.	225 grams
16 oz/1 lb.	455 grams
32 oz/2 lb	900 grams

LIQUID MEASUREMENTS

1/2 fl. oz.	15 ml.	1 tbsp.
1 fl. oz.	30 ml.	1/8 cup
2 fl. oz.	60 ml.	1/4 cup
4 fl. oz.	120 ml.	1/2 cup
8 fl. oz.	240 ml.	1 cup
16 fl. oz.	480 ml.	1 pint

TEMPERATURES

Fahrenheit	Celsius	Gas Mark	Description
32°	0°		
212°	100°		
250°	120°	1/2	
275°	140°	1	Cool
300°	150°	2	
325°	160°	3	Very Moderate
350°	180°	4	Moderate
375°	190°	5	
400°	200°	6	Moderately Hot
425°	220°	7	Hot
450°	230°	8	
475°	240°	9	Very Hot
500°	260°		

PHOTO REFERENCE
(left to right)

GRAN'S KITCHEN

PAGE 12
Sewing Room Entrance Door
Fred & Dulcie, 1996
Dulcie's Kitchen Utensils
Fred's Tomatoes
Fred's Rose Bush, gift to Dulcie
Fred's Catch, 1981
Dulcie's Beads
Milo the Cat
Fred's Kitchen Tea Pot

PAGE 13
Fred's Glasshouse
Bathroom Picture
Field Mushrooms
Fishing Hat
Dulcie's Kitchen Wallpaper
Dulcie, 2008
Fred's Car and Boat
Dulcie's Mum (Susannah Eliza) and
Father (Arthur Charles), 1966
Wood Pile

PAGE 34
Dulcie's Flour Cup
Dulcie's Cheesecake Tray
Dulcie's Kitchen Window
Dulcie's Cooking Table
Fresh Cream and Jam
Dulcie's Favourite Tablecloth
Storage Containers
Cooking Table and Board

Women's Institute Newspaper Article

PAGE 35
Dulcie's Egg Beater
First Women's Institute Committee, 1934
Dilmah Tea Tin
Dulcie's Slice Tin
CWI Celebration Booklet
Dulcie's China
Edmonds Baking Powder Tin
Dulcie's Butter Holder

PAGE 88
Dulcie's Food Essence
Hydrangeas
Dulcie showing Natalie photos
Fred & Dulcie, 1979
Dulcie's old Egg Beater
Fred's 70th with Grandchildren, 1985
Piping Tube
Dance at Weymouth Hall, 1960

PAGE 89
Fred & Dulcie's Wedding Cake
Crocheted Tablecloth
China Tea Set
One of Dulcie's Cookbooks
Cake Forks
Dulcie's Sifter
Fred & Dulcie on Cruise Ship, 1973
PAGE 106
Dulcie's Colander and Mothers Apron

ACKNOWLEDGEMENTS

In true Gran fashion, the making of this book has been a social activity, involving lots of people. First of all, of course, Gran herself, Dulcie May Booker – without her personality, memories and recipes, this book simply would not exist.

My sister Michelle Burrell lent her expertise in food preparation and styling to this project – her talent for chefing is the most obvious indication that "food runs in our family". Her support and encouragement have also been vital.

Master-of-all-trades Sally Greer took the photographs, designed the book and is the associate publisher. Her inspiring spirit of unflappable determination has made my dream a reality.

My Mum, Heather Burrell, is my rock. Even though she's living far away, she has made fantastic efforts to contribute recipes, reminiscences and support to this project – all of which have been greatly appreciated.

Other friends and family have supported me with wonderful encouragement, ideas and opinions. Especial thanks goes to those who contributed recipes: Granny Barr; Grandma Ettena, via my wonderful friend and sister-in-law April, who baked the banana nut bread in the photograph on page 22; Gran's friend Flo; and my cherished Nana Rita.

Geoff Blackwell who inspired me to stay true my vision.

Editor Janet McAllister worked diligently to meet some tight deadlines. I look forward to working with her again.

My daughter Gabrielle has been incredibly patient and supportive during the making of this book.

Always saving the best until last, I want to acknowledge my best friend and my soul mate, my husband Adam who has enabled me to be the woman I want to be. For this I am forever grateful.

NATALIE OLDFIELD

INDEX

Dear Gran and Pop

I love to come to your home and have tea with you.
Your teas are very very very nice   and I love your
fruit salad, and your vegetables Pop. I like your roses Granny.
Thankyou very much for beening a wonderful Gran and Pop.

                    Love from Aaron and Natalie.+++++ooooo